Before Conflict

Preventing Aggressive Behavior

John D. Byrnes

Rowman & Littlefield Education
Lanham • New York • Toronto • Oxford
2002

This title was originally published by ScarecrowEducation. First Rowman & Littlefield Education edition 2008.

Published in the United States of America
by Rowman & Littlefield Education
A Division of Rowman & Littlefield Publishers, Inc.
A wholly owned subsidary of The Rowman & Littlefield Publishing Group, Inc.
4501 Forbes Boulevard, Suite 200, Lanham, Maryland 20706
www.rowmaneducation.com

PO Box 317
Oxford
OX2 9RU, UK

British Library Cataloguing in Publication Information Available

Library of Congress Cataloging-in-Publication Data

Byrnes, John D., 1945–
    Before conflict : preventing aggressive behavior / John D. Byrnes.
       p.   cm.
    "A ScarecrowEducation book"
    Includes bibliographical references and index.
    ISBN 0-8108-4398-6 (alk. paper) — ISBN 0-8108-4397-8 (pbk. : alk. paper)
    1. Aggressiveness.   2. Aggressiveness—Prevention.   3. Violence—Prevention.   4. Persuasion (Psychology)   I. Title.
    BF575.A3 B97   2002
    302.5'4—dc21   2002005359

I wish to dedicate this book to my wife, Frances.
If it where not for her love,
support and tireless editing
this book would not have been completed.

Contents

Copyright and Trademark Statement

Foreword

John Byrnes is a world-class trainer and thinker in the realm of work-place and school violence. Now he has put his tremendous expertise into a book, and never was this book more needed.

Consider:

- What is the single most heinous, horrendous international terrorist act in history? What is the single greatest body count, in a single incident, ever achieved by any non-governmental agency not in time of war? The World Trade Center attack on September 11, 2001. Not some ancient history. Not some distant land. Us. Now.
- What is the single most heinous, horrendous domestic terrorist act in American history? What is the single greatest body count ever achieved in a terrorist act on American soil by an American Citizen? The Oklahoma City bombing. Not some ancient history. Not some distant land. Us. Now.
- What is the single greatest body count ever achieved by any juvenile mass murderer in history? Columbine High School. Prior to Columbine, the "Guinness world record" juvenile mass murder was in my hometown of Jonesboro, Arkansas, where two boys, aged 11 and 13, gunned down 15 students and teachers. Not some ancient history. Not some distant land. Us. Now.

I served as a consultant, on standby as an expert witness in the McVeigh case, and I can tell you that from one very useful and power-ful perspective, Timothy McVeigh was seen as a disgruntled govern-ment employee. He believed that he had been "disrespected" by his nation, and he was going to teach it a lesson.

The only major difference between the school killer and the work-place killer is the age of the killer. In our schools (which are the "work-place" for kids) we are seeing mass murders by students at ages never before seen. We hope that we are wrong; we pray that we are wrong, but we fear that the generation of children who are committing these mass murders in school will be the most violent generation ever when they hit the workplace.

The May 2002 mass murder by a 19-year-old, who expressed his conflict by killing 17 teachers and students in Germany, is an indication of how this trend is progressing. Germany has some of the strictest gun laws, demonstrating that no one is safe and no place is immune. (If we count him as a juvenile, then he has the new record for teen mass mur-der, eclipsing Columbine; and by the time you read this, his "high score" may have been beaten by yet another mass murderer.) As this generation grows older, those who turn to violence will be dedicated to racking up higher and higher scores, it is therefore vital that we prevent aggressive behavior, *before conflict*.

Understand that the vast majority of Americans, and the vast major-ity of our kids, are good people. The teenage pregnancy rate is down. Teen alcohol use is down. Teen drug use is down. Male juvenile vio-lence rates are down, but female rates are skyrocketing. Overall, the current generation of youth is a notch or two better than they have been in a while. But the ones who are bad are very bad, committing mass murders at ages and in numbers never seen before in history.

If just one child in a million commits a mass murder, the result is dozens of juvenile mass murders per year. And if just one employee in a million commits a mass murder, the result is over a hundred mass murders each year. Just a few decades ago the incidence of school mas-sacres was zero, and workplace massacres were quite rare. Today work-place violence is a major and legitimate concern, and the incidence of school violence predicts that the situation will only get worse.

Whether it is the angry child or the angry adult, there is a new twist to terrorism: It's called body count. Whether the perpetrators are school killers, workplace killers or international terrorists, they are not inter-ested in negotiating; their only goal is to kill as many people as humanly possible.

Shaken awake by the horror of recent events, our citizens will no longer sit by as innocent men, women, and children die en masse. We saw this new thinking on September 11, 2001, when Americans on the fourth airplane, Flight 93 over Pennsylvania, fought back. We saw it when passengers on a flight from Paris to Boston subdued a man after he tried to blow up a mix of explosives in his sneakers. And we saw it after the Columbine massacre when police agencies across the country developed "rapid response" techniques to fight against young killers in the halls of our schools.

Now workplace leaders have joined the ranks of those who are dedicating themselves to preparing for and (most importantly) preventing aggression and violence. The problem seems overwhelming, but there is a very useful model to use in our attempt to deal with this problem, and that is the model of fire prevention.

Consider:

- How many children were killed or seriously injured by school fires in the U.S. in the last five years? Answer: Zero. In the workplace the numbers are also comparatively low. Yet we do fire drills and have alarms and sprinklers for something that is only an infinitely remote possibility. And it is because we dedicate all this energy to prevention and preparation that these numbers are so very low.
- How many kids were killed or injured by school violence in the U.S. in the last five years? Answer: according to the U.S. Secret Service study on school violence, in 1998 alone there were 35 murders and over a quarter of a million serious injuries. The numbers of violent acts in the workplace are also very high, and the school violence today predicts a frightening increase in the years to come.

The possibility of a student or employee being seriously injured by violence is fairly low, but it is thousands of times more likely than the possibility of being injured by a fire. And we have the moral obligation to do at least as much preparation for a shooting as for a fire.

That is what this book is all about: a systematic, comprehensive aggression prevention methodology taught by a true world-class expert. Thus I strongly recommend that you not just read but study this excellent and timely book.

Stay safe, stay staunch, and stay ready.

DAVE GROSSMAN
Lt. Col., U.S. Army (ret.)

Author of the Pulitzer Prize–nominated book: *On Killing: The Psychological Cost of Learning to Kill in War and Society*, author of *Stop Teaching our Kids to Kill*, and director of the Killology Research Group (www.killology.com)

Preface

There are two ways to read this book.

You can read *Before Conflict* as you would any other book, straight through from cover to cover. All the material through chapter 8 applies to managing aggression in general, and will benefit you regardless of your career role in the public or private sector.

Chapters 9 through 13 focus on several working environments where aggression has been perceived to be more prevalent, either because of existing statistics or because of recent headlines spotlighting acts of violence in those environments, or both.

Accordingly, the other way to read *Before Conflict* is to begin with a chapter that may deal directly with your working environment. You may be a human resources specialist in the health care industry or social services, a law enforcement official, a principal or guidance counselor in a public school system, a supervisor with the United States Postal Service or the owner/manager of one or more restaurants. So you may prefer to go at once to the chapter that deals specifically with the types of aggression you must deal with on a continuing basis. But regardless of which chapter may be appropriate to your organization, you may want to then proceed to chapter 15, "Aggression's Effect on Productivity," to understand how the level of aggression your people are experiencing is impacting *your* productivity.

If you're a "straight-through" reader, you'll discover some of the same methodologies discussed several times. That occasional overlap is not an oversight. It's because some industry-specific chapters are likely to be read by some readers who may intentionally skip other chapters.

However you read this book, you will discover immediately that it deals with aggression in a new and innovative way. *Before Conflict* will prepare you with the skills you need to recognize the early signs of mounting aggression, and to *prevent* incidents of aggression that may endanger you and your co-workers and that cost your organization in its effectiveness, productivity and hard dollars every working day.

Acknowledgments

The author wishes to thank a whole host of individuals who have participated in the evolution of Aggression Management. Starting with Jim Bullard, whose writing style and influence can be felt throughout this book; Michael A. Cipollaro, whose wisdom, expertise and financial support helped immeasurably in the growth of a fledging business; Dr. Robert A. Evans and Dr. Alan Smolowe, whose help, enthusiasm and training assistance encouraged the evolution of Aggression Management; Scott Clark, whose legal assistance throughout this evolutionary process has been an invaluable asset; John and Donna Painter, Anne and Tony Lunt, Valerie and Roberts Davis for their support and friendship; the Bakely's Breakfast Club who provided friendship and a sounding board filled with wisdom and humor; especially Don Palladeno, Vernon Edger, Jr., Jim Huckeba, Bill McCormick, Ray Srour, Jimmy Goff, Joe Carlisle, Charlotte Dutton, Rev. Charles Cloy, and Bill Coleman. A special thanks to James Younger, former police chief of Winter Park, Florida, and now private investigator, par excellence. It was Jim's query and encouragement that started me on the path of Aggression Management.

Introduction

Anxiety looms over us in our office cubicles, industrial loading docks, when coming out of the supermarket and even in our school classrooms and playgrounds. Whatever happened to America?

I'm talking about that not-so-long-ago country of neat and shady neighborhoods and sturdy brick schools, where folks seemed to be so civil and patient and forgiving, and courtesy really *was* common. I don't mean back in the Eisenhower years, but in *your* recent memory.

If by some time machine an American living in 1979 or even midway through the Reagan administration was suddenly handed a recent copy of *USA Today*, he or she would be dumbfounded at what contemporary Americans are doing to themselves.

School massacres. Drive-by shootings. Road rage. Air rage. Office bombings. Terrorist attacks. Children killing children. Multiple murders by disgruntled employees. Has *anyone* noticed our national madness? And more important, is there no way to control the Great American Anger that can erupt in your workplace, at the ballgame, in your child's classroom, on the highway, or, in tragic cliché, in your neighborhood post office?

Several years ago, I realized that experts in several related fields—criminology, psychology, sociology, biology, anthropology—were trying to get a handle on this emerging American phenomenon. In the media, especially after each well publicized shooting of innocents, it was categorized as "violence in the workplace." (I realized early on that many related incidents, which happen every day and go unreported, are neither violent nor occur where we work.) Books on crisis management, conflict resolution, self-defense, and how to deal with "sudden and unexpected violence" began to fill the store shelves.

Prior to entering this field, I enjoyed a successful career in real estate development. During that time, I consciously honed my skills in negotiation and interpersonal communications, what I call "verbal persuasion." At the same time, over the past 35 years, I've developed proficiency in several of the martial arts. From these two seemingly unrelated areas, I learned that seizing control of a situation, whether in the conference room or on the grappling mat, is a process that one should begin at the first moment of personal contact.

In addition, from years of fascination with and study in many areas of human behavior, I knew that physical violence is not as sudden as it is often portrayed, and need not be unexpected. Instead, it is the climactic eruption of a molten convergence of many factors—physiological, emotional and temporal forces within and beyond the violent individual. Angry employees, jilted lovers and camouflaged predators do not explode from benign to ballistic in a few seconds.

Some experts tackled the topic of "violence in the workplace" from the top down, focusing on how to negotiate with, dissuade and defuse an individual who has already pulled a gun or thrown a punch. Others began at the lower end of the scale, concentrating on how to cope with day-to-day job and personal stress before it got the upper hand.

The more I studied the phenomenon of violence and its precursors, the more I realized that the word "violence" causes us to miss the mark. It generates a *reactive* response to a problem requiring a *preventive* approach. Notice that I did not say *proactive*. One can be *proactively reactive* and that is not acceptable. We must *prevent!* I also saw that many Americans do not take the issue seriously because no *violence* has occurred where they work. They do not realize that the frustrated co-worker, with unhappy home life and money problems, passed over for promotion and beginning to miss work, is cultivating a potential for violence of which he or she might not even be aware.

Accordingly, I began to categorize this spectrum of anger with the term "aggression." As a much more encompassing term, aggression can be expressed in actions that range from slamming a door at the office to murdering the boss. More important, as you are about to learn, aggression is measurable, and if you can measure aggression, you can manage aggression. Aggression can be an angry finger pointed in the air—or on the trigger.

Regardless of the level of aggression, one element slips like a quiet thread of continuity from stress headache to homicide: adrenaline. So, over the course of this book, we will explore the interrelationship of how an aggressor will act, and how a potential victim will respond, based on the flow of this primal chemical element.

In developing the methodology that became the Arts of Aggression Management, I discovered that *aggression is a progressive continuum.* As such it demands appropriate responses from an intended victim at each point on that continuum—and *not* just in the instant before violence occurs. Since 1993, when I founded the Center for Aggression Management, the world around us has grown more dangerous. The bombing of the Murrow Building in Oklahoma City brought floor after floor crashing down on a daycare center, killing dozens, including 19 children. The World Trade Center was attacked by terrorists. School shooters have murdered a growing number of young people whose only mistake was being in school. Angry former employees have returned to retail stores, insurance offices and government agencies to kill their former supervisors and anyone else who happened by.

Because violence is so unpleasant, we often deny its potential in our own lives by ignoring the warning signs. We override intuition, dismiss evidence and repeat the comforting mantra that it can't happen here and it will not happen to me. Facing the possibility of rage takes almost as much resolve as facing rage itself. Finally, after so many children have been laid to rest, school officials around the country are realizing that *it* can in fact happen anywhere. The same is true of employers in a growing number of industries.

Accordingly, in seminar after seminar, I've been asked to set down the crux of Aggression Management methodologies in book form, for widest distribution to office workers, security personnel, law enforcement officers, educators, plant supervisors, or anyone else who may be thrust into a confrontation—or may even notice the potential for a confrontation.

And that is what I have done. This book is for you.

We will begin by examining the scope of aggression and its impact on society, business productivity and even the national economy. Then we'll define and discuss the nature of aggression, its origins, and its well-defined continuum. Having learned the nature of the beast, we'll spend some time learning the skills of the Arts of Aggression Management. Then we'll talk about aggression in the schools and in the public service sector where personal contact with a cross-section of often-volatile individuals is all in a day's work. (In fact, the Center for Aggression Management originated as the Florida Law Enforcement Training Academy, teaching police officers how to manage aggression in both themselves and their suspects in custody.)

Through this book, I want to move public discourse beyond the current cacophony of confusion and recrimination about this epidemic of aggressive behavior and provide a catalyst for solutions. On a more individual level, I hope to open a window through which you can identify more clearly the features of aggression as it moves from its alpha (anxiety and stress) to omega (violence) stage. And since the term Aggression *Management* implies taking action, I also acquaint you with the skills you may need to intervene confidently against aggression anywhere along the path of its gathering momentum. It will be my objective to convince you to become an *Aggression Manager*, an individual who manages aggression in others and in themselves. This is an individual who is empowered with the skills of identifying the emergence of aggression, is able to foresee the possibility of conflict, and has the ability and sense of responsibility to engage and prevent aggression before it becomes conflict. If already embroiled in aggression, an Aggression Manager understands how to defuse aggression or, if needed, how to effectively intervene in a way so as to minimize harm and expense.

But the window through which you examine aggression is also a mirror. As you learn to look out, you need to study your own reflection as well, so that you can be prepared when the time comes to step forward and be part of the solution. There are several reasons for you to do this. First, if you do not take control of a deteriorating employee situation or an unfolding incident of aggression who will? Second, your initiation of proper, measured action will minimize your organization's and your own risk of assault and resulting litigation.

Finally, at a deeper level, I want you to look into your own soul as the person you are. What if the unthinkable occurred? What if an incident exploded in your area, involving your people, and resulted in the death of one of those who looked to you for leadership? Could you live with yourself in the knowledge that you *could* have done something but did not, or would not? Sure, an investigation might exonerate you legally based on available evidence, but *you would know*. And you wouldn't let yourself off quite as easily. The rest of your life is a long time to be gnawed by the dark truth that *you,* however unwittingly, were at least partially responsible for the death of an innocent. It is a burden I wouldn't want to wish on anyone. But it *is* an uncertain, dangerous world, and you *must* be prepared.

I cannot teach you the courage to take the responsibility your newly acquired skills confer. You must look yourself in the eye and seek that courage yourself.

Or else, for all your newfound knowledge, you will continue to be part of the problem.

Chapter 1

Aggression—A Social Epidemic

During a period in which violent crime, such as murder and armed robbery, is actually decreasing, a phenomenon I call social aggression is increasing to epidemic proportions. At first glance, this could be considered a natural consequence of the country's urbanization, and written off as a necessary evil of progress. After all, the crowds, the rush and bustle of city life all tend to depersonalize other people and reduce individuals to obstacles. Ask any out-of-towner just returned from any major city.

But nowadays, aggression in its ultimate extreme—homicidal violence—is just as likely to detonate in Mississippi as Manhattan. The outbreak of school shootings beginning in the late nineties didn't occur in large cities or even inner cities, but in heartland communities of Kentucky, Arkansas, Montana and Colorado.

We will describe and discuss the nature of aggression in the following chapter, but since this entire book requires you to understand "aggression," and differentiate it from "violence," let us look up what *Webster's* has to say: "*Aggression—an unprovoked attack . . . forceful, attacking behavior . . . destructively hostile to others or to oneself*"

Nowhere does *Webster's* specify "physical attack" or "physical violence" as a requisite for aggression. You can find yourself the victim of aggression just driving around town any day of the week. You don't have to dodge in and out of traffic, just drive 45 mph in a 45-mph speed zone. Look in the rearview mirror. Aggression erupts behind you immediately.

The scope of aggression, like a pebble in a pond, ripples outward from your own experiences to encompass the whole country. Consider these figures compiled in 2000 by the United States Department of Justice:

- About two million employees were attacked at jobs across the country. These attacks ranged from slaps or kicks to fatal shootings.
- 1,000 employees were killed (Occupational Safety and Health Administration).
- Each day, an estimated 16,400 threats are made, 723 workers are attacked and 43,800 are harassed (Workplace Violence Research Institute).

These numbers fluctuate from year to year. Whether the number of killings in our workplace are 1,000 or 600, there are far too many innocents dying in our workplaces, schools and across the spectrum of our society.

The National Institute for Occupational Safety and Health (NIOSH) reported that at the end of the twentieth century *each week* some 20 people are murdered and another 18,000 assaulted while working or on duty in the United States. This figure includes the robbery/murder of taxi drivers, gas station attendants, store clerks and fast food employees, as well as physical assaults which are actually reported by the victim. How many more were not reported?

Medical expenses, workers' compensation claims, loss of productivity, litigation, out-of-court settlements and absenteeism by employees who called in "sick" to avoid returning to a threatening work environment combined to cost American employers $4.2 *billion*, according to the National Safe Workplace Institute. I recently learned that the Royal Mail in the United Kingdom suffers a cost of £247 million each year due to "employee friction" which results in employee absenteeism and lost productivity. What the Royal Mail identified and measured was that when you have aggressors in your organization, no one else wants to be there. These aggressors cause tardiness and absenteeism (sick days) and finally they cause turnover, and you lose good people who are so expensive to replace and train. In so many ways, then, there is a hard dollar cost of aggression in virtually every organization.

Need some more statistics? At the end of 1999, the Society for Human Resource Management (SHRM) received responses to a survey on violent incidents from more than a thousand corporations. Here are some of the results:

- 57% reported violent incidents over the past 12 months, up from 48% in 1996 and 33% in 1993 (Notice the increase of aggression, not the decrease of aggression)
- 78% had violent incidents for organizations with 250 or more employees
- 73% had equipped with security systems to control access (What does this say about security systems?)
- 97% were not what we see in the media like shooting, knifings and sexual assaults, they were verbal threats to fist fights (This 97% is where we must focus our attention to affect prevention in our organization)
- Effects on employees (Here illustrated is the cost of aggression in your organization)
  - Increased stress: 43%
  - Increased fear: 31%
  - Decreased productivity: 23%
  - Decreased co-worker trust: 22%
  - Decreased morale: 18%
  - Increased absenteeism: 9%
  - Increased turnover: 6%
- 2% were individuals with criminal histories

The last statistic, taken from a previous SHRM survey, is particularly significant. In case we might smugly characterize aggressors as habitual troublemakers or sociopaths with a history of assaults, this figure tells us that 98% of the aggressors reported in this survey *had no criminal history!* They were ordinary citizens, many with families and mortgages, who, under seemingly ordinary circumstances, became aggressive and, in many cases, attacked a fellow employee.

So, in a raging national epidemic of aggression, just who is likely to "go ballistic" given the right circumstances? The guy in the next office. The polite kid on the loading dock. The elderly gent in the stock room. Even the quiet administrative assistant you had to let go last week.

Women are especially vulnerable to aggression. The U.S. Bureau of Labor Statistics reports that homicide is the leading cause of job-related deaths for women; and the second leading cause of job-related deaths for men.

As I was writing this very chapter, the owner of a small electronics business in Orlando dismissed the furor over aggression in the workplace as other peoples' problem. Over lunch one day, he said, "We don't hire people who have any hint of trouble in their resume, or who raise even the shadow of a doubt during the interview process. Then we pay well, and reward for exceptional work. I can tell you, we have 26 happy, stable, productive women. A family, really. That is how we keep all that stuff from happening in our shop."

"What about their spouses?" I asked. "What about their boyfriends? Did you check them out too?"

The owner's eyes widened. "What for?"

"Because women have been assaulted or killed at work by a husband or boyfriend who barges into a nice business like yours and starts shooting. A guy under a judge's restraining order not to return to the home still knows where his wife or girlfriend works, and that she has to be there during certain hours. She's a sitting duck. And she's sitting in your place."

"Well, our women are all smart and level-headed. They're married to good men. In fact, I know most of the husbands."

"How many of these women are single?"

"About a dozen."

"Do you know who they're dating now? And how many former boyfriends have these 12 girls accumulated? And why did they break up?"

He shrugged, indicating he had no answers.

"How could you know, right? So you're operating in a state of denial that keeps you from being prepared in case, just in case, one angry guy storms in one day to show his girl who's boss, and shoots holes in your happy little corporate family."

I was hard on this self-assured business owner because he is a long-time friend. But I also wanted to drive home the point that complacency about workplace aggression is the worst enemy of being prepared for it. Incidentally, as the above scenario illustrates, this is not a gender-neutral issue. Although I don't discount the wrath of angry female employees, throughout this book, with no apologies, I characterize the aggressor as male. That is because many statistics show that up to 95% of all aggressors are men.

As I discuss in a later chapter, the growing incidents of aggression are not confined to the workplace, but are becoming more and more common in America's schools as well. The Longitudinal Study of Selected School Districts, conducted by Research Triangle Institute in 1997, revealed that 37% of 8th and 9th grade students were afraid of attacks at school. And that figure reflects student fears *before* the rash of school shootings that culminated in the Columbine High School massacre in 1999 and continue today. The Ethics of American Youth, 2000 Report Card, conducted by the non-profit, non-partisan Josephson Institute of Ethics, released April 2000, revealed that 39% of middle school students and 36% of high school students say they don't feel safe at school. 43% of high school and 37% of middle school boys believe it is OK to hit or threaten a person who makes them angry. 75% of all boys and over 60% of girls surveyed said they hit someone in the past 12 months because they were angry. More than one in five (21%) high schools boys and 15% of middle school males took a weapon to school at least once in the past year. We have been informed by the U.S. Secret Service, in their Safe School Initiative report in October 2000, "There is no accurate or useful profile of the school shooter, nor for assessing the risk that a particular student may pose for school-based targeted violence." Students are not the only individuals that are dropping out. There have been numerous articles across the country that declare the epidemic of teachers leaving. They chronicle individuals like Jeanne Heath who quit after 22 years explaining she fears students who seemed increasingly bitter and dangerous. It is estimated that states like Mississippi could lose as much as 70% of their teachers to retirement within the next five years. I continue to hear that new teachers are being placed in the most difficult and dangerous schools where they soon become discouraged and leave the profession. With fewer individuals becoming teachers and more individuals leaving the teaching profession, who is going to teach your children, or your children's children?

The aggression around us stems no doubt from many causes. Depending on who we listen to, these causes include a more permissive culture, a lower threshold of gratuitous violence created by the entertainment industry, a breakdown of the traditional family unit, the apathy of some public schools in addressing aggression—the list goes on and on.

Rather than unduly focusing on who is to blame or why we have evolved into such an aggressive society, I want to deal with the evolution of human aggression, to teach and prepare you as one person to identify the emergence of aggression and foresee the possibility of conflict, so that you will be able to engage and prevent aggression before it becomes conflict. Perhaps, in this way, we can effect societal change—one person at a time.

Aside from the fact that we live and work in an aggressive environment, other factors contribute to this crisis of aggression. One is the transition of corporate America from one culture to another. Twenty years ago, we still had a corporate landscape of large and stable corporations, offering employees the reasonable assurance of 30 years of employment, a gold watch and pension. Then, one by one, companies realized that if they were to compete in the emerging global marketplace, boost profitability and make stockholders happy, they had to streamline operations from the mailroom to the boardroom. Euphemisms such as "downsizing," "rightsizing" and "restructuring" became code words for the layoff of many thousands of Americans who had assumed job security.

Many turned their sudden unemployment into opportunities to forge their own careers in small business. Like acorns shaken from some great corporate oak, they sprouted new companies, hungry to compete and succeed. A new generation of entrepreneurs, especially at the dawn of the Internet Age, launched into cyberspace. The effect of this remaking of business has been healthy for many Americans.

Unfortunately, countless thousands of others have been left behind. Unable to retrain into new technologies, and tossed by a sea of change into uncertainty, they've had to cling to the driftwood that had been their lifeboat of security. Instead of being buoyed by optimism and opportunity, they've become fearful of their future, and embittered by what they see as betrayal of a career-long covenant.

The result has been a substructure of workers who see themselves as victims of "the system," and harbor a free-floating grudge further feeding their insecurity. As we've seen in the statistics, these are not criminals or society's misfits. These are by and large good people whose fear has spawned undercurrents of suspicion and hostility. They are quite often faithful employees whose sense of fairness has been violated by new policies, the advent of new technologies or new supervisors who do not appreciate their years of loyalty. Given day-to-day circumstances, their feelings can become manifested in absenteeism, tardiness, poor performance and continuous complaining. Then, one day, they seethe and bubble into open aggression or even violence. No wonder the workplace aggressor is all too often a male over the age of 35, a long-time employee who feels threatened by his company, his boss and especially younger co-workers who may seem to be pushing him aside.

Yet another contributing factor is job stress. The gurus of technology assured us all that the emerging developments in automation and telecommunications would make our jobs easier. We would live in a paperless society with more free time and a better quality of life. For most workers, that rosy projection has wilted in the heat of greater than ever workplace pressure. The computer, fax machine, teleconferencing and email have not *cut* our workload, but compressed it to become more demanding! Jobs that took three days to turn around are now expected to be done in hours.

The result for workers is higher levels of stress, frustration and anger at simply not having the time to devote to tasks. These workers are being pressed to perform faster, but with the same level of quality. Once again, chronic stress can explode anytime into aggression. Stress and aggression are inexorably connected. What begins as mounting stress all too often leads to aggression. So learning to manage aggression is learning to manage stress.

Substance abuse is another catalyst of workplace aggression. In addition to illegal drugs that pervade our society, the pharmaceutical industry has developed an enormous cabinet of prescription medications to relax or energize, and otherwise alter the chemical balances that constrict and influence how we behave.

But humans are still humans, many of whom assume that if a little of a good thing feels good, a lot will feel even better. In a growing number of cases, reckless abuse follows recommended use, with unpredictable results that can impact co-workers or classmates. The casual passing of pills among school friends has caused concerned administrators to prohibit students from even bringing aspirin to school for a headache. But whether it is prescribed medication or heroin, substance abuse leads even untroubled individuals down unexplored paths of behavior with dark byways of potential aggression.

Finally, the availability of guns has helped make America the most violent society in modern history. (A purpose of this book, by the way, is not to debate the morality of firearms, but rather to acknowledge their role as an accessible tool for moving aggression into the realm of physical violence.) Guns in the hands of angry, frustrated, unstable aggressors, legally and illegally, are killing supervisors, co-workers and school children. Guns are pervasive in American society, so their use as weapons of choice for aggressors is only likely to increase in the years ahead. While we focus on guns, let us not forget about bombs. Violence requires three things: means, motive and an opportunity. Lt. Col. Dave Grossman, a world-renowned expert on school violence and author of *Stop Teaching Our Kids to Kill*, tells us that this form of domestic terrorism is on the rise perpetrated by pint-size mass murderers who are as young as 11 years old. They have the "means" (Internet) and the "motive" (media fame) to build and use the bombs. They are also "scripted" by the violent video games, "mass murder simulators," which almost all include extensive use of bombs as "rewards" to get a "high score." At this writing, there are two reported bomb incidents in schools in British Columbia, Canada. Even in Canada, where gun laws are particularly strict, there is a serious problem with this emerging threat.

The complexities of dealing with aggression are compounded by a labyrinth of government laws and guidelines, mandates and court rulings, and we are living in the most litigious society in the world.

In the past, an employer could ask a job prospect any question, thoroughly investigate the individual and check with past references for performance. That employer could also fire an employee on a suspicion that he was a potential threat, with few or no repercussions. If an employee was injured or killed in workplace violence, seldom did the employer incur any liability for not having taken steps to prevent that violence. The feeling about the aggressor was, "The guy was just no good. There was nothing anybody could have done."

Today, by contrast, the individual rights of employees often supercede the rights of an employer to protect all employees. Even some of the most effective methods of preventing workplace aggression are either prohibited by law, or can be grounds for a lawsuit.

For example, should a previous employer provide a damaging reference about a job prospect, that employer can be sued for slander. Administering applicants a psychological test may be seen as an invasion of privacy.

If an employer reduces an employee's status due to emotional instability, that action may violate the Americans with Disabilities Act.

After all these restraints against an employer using due diligence, in situations where an employee becomes violent, that employer may well become liable for whatever injuries or deaths may occur. For the employer, this is a horrendous "Catch-22."

With all the survey figures that substantiate the aggression epidemic, most Americans become aware of it only after a heartbreaking multiple homicide makes the evening news. The news media, in fact, has contributed to a skewed public image of violence. The United States Postal Service, with 830,000 employees, has received nationwide network coverage of its various shootings to the point that "going postal" has entered the American vernacular. Yet the percentage per capita of postal employees involved in acts of workplace violence is significantly lower than those in most other industries. "Going postal" is a myth but the media continues to perpetuate this mantra.

By contrast, thousands of anonymous employees every working day are cursed, intimidated, harassed, humiliated, punched, beaten, raped and otherwise assaulted by co-workers in incidents that are never even reported to supervisors, let alone the press.

There would be many more additional incidents that would boost the statistics we've cited except they are cloaked in the silence of fearful victims and witnesses of aggression. Much like domestic violence in the home environment, workplace aggression is still often the "family secret" of American business. It is an untidy issue that many company managers are still tiptoeing around, hoping it won't occur, and not sure of what to do if it does.

What companies do recognize is that there are no hard, fast "rules of engagement." Every incident of aggression is unique, with an infinite number of variables, requiring subjective judgments to be made quickly and, it is hoped, correctly.

In order to help dissipate this fog of uncertainty, I founded the Center for Aggression Management. Calling on years of experience, research and analysis, I developed a comprehensive methodology that is the heart of this book.

Wherever they work, live or play, individuals who have learned the Arts of Aggression Management (I call them Aggression Managers) are now empowered to step forward and resolve whatever incidents occur or, even more important, to foresee them and prevent their occurrence. This elusive issue has at last been given a handle, a proactive means of reducing and even preventing aggression, helping to bring this nation's tragic aggression epidemic under control.

Having examined the scope of aggression, and its effect on our national psyche, let us now turn our focus on its multifaceted nature, and on what I call the Aggression Continuum.

CHAPTER 2

The Nature of Aggression

Since 1993, I have conducted a continuous study into the nature of aggression in humans, and have concluded that one cannot get to the concept of aggression prevention through the use of the word *violence*, i.e., *workplace violence, school violence, societal violence.* Typically, *violence* conjures up fatality, violent crime and physical assault, which causes two problems. First, those who have not experienced or witnessed violence for themselves all too often consider it a non-issue, at least until violence actually occurs. Second, when looking for a solution to *violence*, we tend to come up with Crisis Management—"I have a crisis and I need to manage it!" This is reactionary only! We, therefore, cannot achieve aggression prevention if we focus on the word *violence*.

If our responsibility is the safety of those in our organization or our family, isn't it essential that we prevent hazard as opposed to waiting to react to it? If all we intend to do is to react to aggression we will, eventually, be confronted with physical violence. Yet, outside of Aggression Management, the only method of dealing with aggression and violence today is conflict resolution, which *presupposes* conflict. You're already reacting, you're already past any opportunity to prevent aggression and thereby violence.

As we enter into this new century we need a paradigm shift, a shift from reacting to aggression and violence to a paradigm of aggression prevention. As you can see from the news headlines, current methods for preventing aggression and violence in our workplaces, in our schools and in our society are not working!

When we look at conventional means of managing aggression, we see topics like *conflict resolution, anger management* and *managing our feelings.*

Conflict resolution presupposes conflict. So those who are only trained to respond verbally when two individuals are in conflict (nose-to-nose) will eventually have to deal with someone who only communicates physically instead of verbally. Suddenly out of nowhere, that person strikes out. God forbid they have a weapon and they pull the trigger.

An example of this was a school shooting that occurred in Lake Worth, Florida. A young boy stood up in class, faced his teacher and fired one shoot, striking his teacher in the face and killing him on the spot. Everyone was shocked. This boy was a straight A student and an amicable young man. But he expressed his *conflict* that day by pulling the trigger. Since there were no teachers or administrators looking for the warning signs *before* conflict they were not able to foresee this horrible act.

The other conventional approach to aggression and violence is *anger management*. The reason that this approach fails is due to an axiom of management: *if you can measure it, you can manage it.* The problem with *anger management* is that we all measure anger differently and therefore experience and express it differently. There is no common denominator or metric for us to measure, and thereby manage anger.

The final conventional approach is *managing our feelings.* Articulating our feelings accurately can often elude us. It is a complex, convoluted process to identify and understand our feelings, much less accurately express them. It is even more difficult to identify, understand and express the feelings of others. Think about one of the most popular sitcoms: *Frasier.* Here are two brothers, both psychiatrists, attempting to express their feelings to each other, to roars of laughter. And the greatest laughter comes when their father, an ex-cop, yells at them "cut the crap." Humans, men especially, hesitate to express their feelings; much less articulate them as a means of dealing with aggression.

We will demonstrate in this chapter how to identify the emergence of aggression and foresee the possibility of conflict. In our next chapters we will share with you the skills to engage and diffuse aggression, whether in someone else or in yourself. These two elements of the basic Aggression Continuum are crucial to effective Aggression Management. To identify the emergence of aggression, in itself, is not enough; you must *foresee the possibility of conflict.* Embedded within that *foresee-ability* is the sense of urgency and the motivation to do something and do it now! Following this we'll demonstrate an effective means to *measure* aggression whether in others or in ourselves.

To accomplish these goals we will introduce you to the basic Aggression Continuum (Figure 2.1). This is a graphic that illustrates that aggression is made up of parts; and if you understand these parts and you learn the appropriate skills that are provided in this book, you can diffuse most aggression.

As we look at the Aggression Continuum graphic we see a Trigger Phase, an Escalation Phase and a Crisis Phase. The first lesson we learn from this graphic is that the more we allow an aggressor to escalate, the less opportunity we will have to diffuse him. There will be a point, eventually, where any effort on our part to diffuse the aggressor will be fruitless, but the converse is also true. The sooner we identify the emergence of aggression in an individual, engage and begin the diffusing process the more effective our applied skills will be. Therefore it is our objective to identify the emergence of aggression even at its earliest stage.

Now let's examine more closely each of these phases: the Trigger Phase, the Escalation Phase and the Crisis Phase.

TRIGGER PHASE

In the Trigger Phase, we all experience explosions of anxiety called triggers: we wake up late for work or school; we go in the kitchen for coffee and breakfast and find none; with stomach grumbling, we leave the house, and get to the bottom of the driveway only to find we have forgotten it is garbage day; we jam on our brakes and drag the garbage to the road; now we are late and we have to face the morning traffic! We all experience these triggers but we learn to cope with them.

ESCALATION PHASE

When an individual can no longer cope with his triggered anxiety and as one trigger accumulates upon another, this potential aggressor now

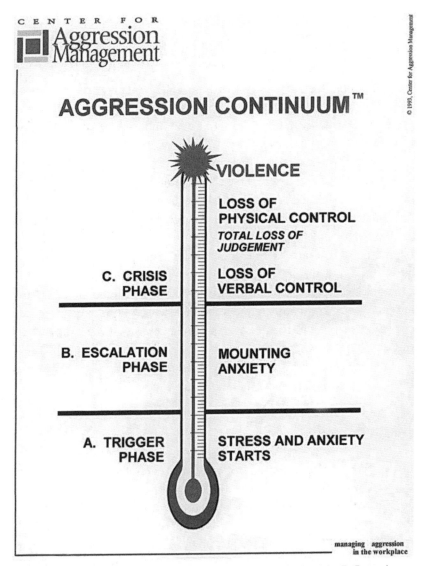

Figure 2.1   *Aggression Continuum, Simple (Created by or for Dr. John D. Byrnes)*

enters the Escalation Phase and mounting anxiety. This mounting anxiety differs from normal "stress and anxiety" because it creates changes that we can identify. These changes become evidenced in three areas: *behavior, body language* and *interpersonal communications*. Obviously, the better you know an individual the more easily you can identify the changes occurring.

Behavior is our first glimpse into the emergence of aggression in others. Aggressive behavior can be something as subtle as scattered and disjointed thinking by one who is normally organized and methodical. This change in behavior should encourage us to engage that person in a genuine and caring manner with "I notice you're a little distracted today. Is anything wrong?" Then you *shut up!* Allowing this person to share his story with you may be defusing what otherwise could become an incident of aggression, *even before it becomes conflict.*

At this point, and for future reference, let's identify the *two driving forces* of aggression.

Primal Aggression Continuum

The Primal Aggression Continuum utilizes forces that are physiological (chemical and neurological) actions the body takes to preserve and protect itself. The civility with which we treat one another in our day-to-day dealings is a veneer that masks those forces—until we feel endangered or threatened, either physically or emotionally. Then that most primal of human chemicals, adrenaline, kicks in naturally in mind and body, triggering the "fight or flight" mode. Primal Aggression is usually described as an individual losing control, whereas Cognitive Aggression is usually the aggression of a predator, a victimizer or a terrorist.

Cognitive Aggression Continuum

Unlike primal aggression reactions that are natural responses in the mind and body, the Cognitive Aggression Continuum describes deliberate and conscious (or non-conscious, i.e., conscious behavior as a child becomes non-conscious as an adult), usually manipulative in nature, to enable the aggressor to achieve and maintain an advantage over "victims" and over any individual who intervenes. Cognitive Aggression, often well planned and always insidious, is a far greater intellectual challenge for the Aggression Manager. Cognitive aggressive behavior progresses through nine stages, which encompass the complete spectrum of aggression. Table 2.1, Cognitive Aggression Continuum, shows that this process starts with hardening. When an individual moves away from a win/win solution and begins to *harden* his position on his issue versus your issues, he is beginning on a path of definable Cognitive Aggression. This course could ultimately result in *plunging together into the abyss,* a culmination of violence to you, those in your care and even to the aggressor himself. Terrorists, whether perpetrated by the al Qaeda on the World Trade Center, a worker returning to his workplace targeting supervisors, a love interest or fellow workers and then himself, or by two young men on their classmates at Columbine High School and then themselves, can transcend through the Cognitive Aggression Continuum and not yet perpetrate physical violence. Either their victim(s) is/are not yet available to them or they have not yet positioned their victim(s) for attack. They are typically far more premeditated in their actions.

We can follow the aggressor's *body language*, what we sometimes call "non-verbal leakage" because these aggressive signals just leak out. Body language is more recognizable and often aggression is escalating as you watch.

The eyes can be one of our first indicators of aggression. Humans do not normally stare at other humans. Humans stare at objects, TVs, paintings, the horizon, etc. So what does it mean when another person begins to stare at you? It means he's turning you into an object. I don't mean the loving gaze of a parent, but the obvious stare of an emerging aggressor. It is not instinctual for one human to attack another. For one human to attack another human, he must detach himself from his victim. One of the first signs of this detachment is when an aggressor begins to stare, or the aggressor make little or no eye contact, often turning his head and eyes downward. This action is often followed by eyebrows frowning, drying mouth, clenched teeth, sweating, veins appearing on the neck and head area and as blood flows to these areas the face turn red with anger. Finally, you may observe the aggressor starting to breathe fast and shallow, beginning to hyperventilate.

Along with behavior and body language, thirdly, we can identify someone in the *Escalation Phase* by the way they communicate with us, or *interpersonal communications.* We call this the *Verbal Aggression Scale.* Aggressors go through a process. By *questioning our authority, refusing* to do what we ask them to do, they *verbally release* or vent on us and finally they make *intimidating* or *threatening* remarks. If nothing is done to stop the escalation the next step on the Verbal Aggression Scale is to cross the Crisis Phase threshold and begin losing complete verbal control. We will discuss the Verbal Aggression Scale in more detail in chapter 6, Pacing the Aggression— Verbal Persuasion.

CRISIS PHASE

As you can see from Figure 2.1 the Crisis Phase begins with the aggressor losing verbal control, then he completely loses his quality of judgment, followed by the detonation of the aggression explosion—the loss of physical control.

Loss of verbal control is evident when verbalization becomes disjointed and then stops. But there is more to observe: direct prolonged eye contact as the aggressor continues turning you into an object as he prepares to attack; moving in and out of your personal space and perhaps even kicking the ground in front of you. Typically an aggressor does not want to get into a fist fight, this would mean blood, torn clothing and broken expensive watches. What he's trying to do is to intimidate his opponent into *submission*. The final loss of verbal control signals are: pursed lips, the baring of teeth and even growling sounds. We'll discuss this primal, almost animalistic behavior in more detail in an upcoming chapter.

As we approach the detonation of the aggression explosion the aggressor loses complete and total quality of judgment and then loses physical control.

I will now introduce you to the body language of an *attacker*—for two reasons. First, knowing this body language offers you the ability to remove yourself as a target. Second, once you have removed yourself as a target, you must now document the incident that has just occurred. Are you going to be able to document in a way that will justify your actions as a professional? Will this documentation enable you to come through this incident professionally unscathed? You must be able to describe, for a reviewing individual, board, commission (or in the worst case, a judge and jury in a court of law) the behavior, body language and the communication of the aggressor in a clear clinical way. Why? To convince whomever you need to that you have acted in a professional way. Some of the body language to look for is:

- The aggressor's head tilts back away from the victim in a further attempt to disconnect with the victim.
- His facial color turns pale as his blood vessels constrict and his blood flow is redirected from his face and hands to the torso area. We call this process vasoconstriction. As the face turns pale with rage, the teeth clench and the facial muscles distort. All these signals are meant to menace and cower the victim.
- Breathing progresses from fast and shallow now to fast and deep.
- The aggressor's hands, due to vasoconstriction, begin pumping, quivering or just clenching, in an unconscious attempt to get blood back into the hands. When confronted by an aggressor it is important to focus on the palms of the hands, not just the hands. If the aggressor has a weapon, he will typically hold and conceal it in the palms of his hands.
- Veins in the arms, neck and facial area that we have noticed before now are bulging.
- Target Glancing. The eyes are often called the "windows to the soul." In an incident of aggression, they are also windows through which we can foresee a physical attack. An attacker will take his eyes from the victim's face and begin looking at intended strike areas, typically the area we refer to as the "lifeline." The lifeline is actually a vital area created when two lines are drawn from each of our eyes, or at the base of the forehead, down our torso to intersect at our groin. This angular area encompasses approximately 85% of all of our vital organs, and instinctively becomes the aggressor's primary strike zone. Finally, watch for the aggressor to make a body shift. The aggressor may turn away, completely disconnecting with his victim before spinning around to attack.

You have now been exposed to the behavior, body language and verbal communication influenced by the body's chemical stimulant of aggression: adrenaline. Now let's examine the cognitive side of aggression— what goes through the mind of an aggressor.

Table 2.1.   Cognitive Aggression Continuum

Phase	No.	Stage	Identifying Aggression in Ourselves	Identifying Aggression in Others	Threshold to Next Level
Crisis Phase	9	Plunging Together into the Abyss	I will destroy the enemy at any and all cost	The Aggressor takes self-destructive action in an attempt to destroy the enemy	Omega
	8	Win/Lose Attack	I will crush the enemy, without becoming a victim in the process	The Aggressor makes vicious attacks to the enemy's vital areas	Aggressor gives up self-preservation
Escalation Phase	7	Limited Destructive Blows	I will demonstrate my potential wrath—I will establish my victim as *the quintessential enemy*	The Aggressor makes declarations and threats which are followed by interrupted communication—complete detachment occurs	Aggressor prepares to attack the enemy's core
	6	Threat Strategies	I will control my victim—I will position him for an attack	The Aggressor presents the ultimatum—he aggressively responds to perceived threats, possibly, on the verge of panic	Aggressor triangulates sanctioned attacks—Aggressor executes ultimatum—righteous indignation
	5	Forced Loss of Face	I will expose & attack my victim publicly—I will unmask my victim as an enemy of his/her community	The Aggressor unmasks his victim as an enemy	Aggressor prepares ultimatum
	4	Image Destruction—Triangulation	I will establish my opponent as a problem—I will *plant a seed of distrust* with those in his/her community	The Aggressor demonstrates *deniable punishment behavior*, issues become bipolar, he attacks the victim's core identities	Aggressor prepares to create loss of face
	3	Communicate with Actions vs. Words	I no longer need to communicate with words, my actions will speak for themselves—I will block any understanding or empathy—I become self-absorbed	The Aggressor takes action without consulting others—the Aggressor appears detached and self absorbed	Aggressor begins attacking victim's image
	2	Debate	I establish my position vs. expressing interests—face to face—Taking "a side"	The Aggressor becomes fixated on his view, competitive and distrustful	Aggressor takes action without consulting others
	1	Hardening	I focus on my issues only—I harden my points of view	The Aggressor becomes more distant, argumentative, lacking understanding & empathy	Aggressor begins to position for winning vs. expressing interests and having a winning rational

As we have said, aggressive behavior follows a linear progression covering nine cognitive stages, which encompass the complete spectrum of aggression. We believe that most humans, during the initial stages, do not realize that they are participating in Cognitive Aggression. To understand the Cognitive Aggression Continuum empowers humans to refrain from this type of aggressive intent, and enhances their ability to guide others in refraining from aggressive behavior.

Referring to the Cognitive Aggression Continuum chart above (Table 2.1), we see that the aggressive process starts at the bottom of the chart with *Hardening*. Moving up from the desirable win/win solution, begins the *hardening* process and the onset of aggression. But before we discuss the nine stages of Cognitive Aggression let's review the column headers and their meanings.

Column 1, "Phase," illustrates the connection with our Aggression Continuum, that template that helps us identify to what degree an aggressor has escalated, offering us the ability to engage and effectively diffuse impending aggression.

Columns 2 and 3 identify and name the nine stages of Cognitive Aggression.

Column 4 has an important title, "Identifying Aggression in Ourselves." This is particularly important because we have identified that aggression and violence is often in direct proportion to how a victim responds with an aggressor! That's right! When you have an aggressor, whose adrenaline is already pumping, it is a natural human response for your adrenaline to rise preparing you for an attack. What are you going to do with your adrenaline? All too often this adrenaline serves to escalate an already bad situation. Many times a situation could have been de-escalated if it were not for the victim's adrenaline taking over, causing that individual to respond in a way that exacerbates the problem. For this reason we must remain vigilant to our own Cognitive Aggression, thereby ensuring that we don't become part of the problem.

Column 5 is titled "Identifying Aggression in Others," which is self-explanatory and will be discussed in detail later.

Column 6 is titled "Threshold to Next Level." This column gives us the opportunity to know whether aggression is static or escalating. By following a described behavior horizontally across from left to right, if you identify behavior described in Column 6, you'll know that this aggressor is escalating and that you must take appropriate actions to encourage de-escalation.

Now let's go back to the column labeled "Identifying Aggression in Ourselves" and examine it vertically from the bottom working our way up to the top. As we escalate up this column we are looking for "intent." Our intent is the first sign of aggression in ourselves. Is our intent in the best interests of this individual or is our intent solely in our own best interests? If the latter is true then we could be escalating on the Cognitive Aggression Continuum.

I would first like to bring your attention to *Debate*: "I establish my position vs. expressing interests." When *I take a position*, I am actually saying "go ahead, try and move me" and this is adversarial, which is

Table 2.2.   Identifying Aggression in Ourselves

Phase	No.	Stage	Identifying Aggression in Ourselves
Crisis Phase	9	Plunging Together into the Abyss	I will destroy the enemy at any and all cost
	8	Win/Lose Attack	I will crush the enemy, without becoming a victim in the process
Escalation Phase	7	Limited Destructive Blows	I will demonstrate my potential wrath—I will establish my victim as *the quintessential enemy*
	6	Threat Strategies	I will control my victim—I will position him for an attack
	5	Forced Loss of Face	I will expose & attack my victim publicly—I will unmask my victim as an enemy of his/her community
	4	Image Destruction— Triangulation	I will establish my opponent as a problem—I will *plant a seed of distrust* with those in his/her community
	3	Communicate with Actions vs. Words	I no longer need to communicate with words, my actions will speak for themselves—I will block any understanding or empathy—I become self-absorbed
	2	Debate	I establish my position vs. expressing interests—face to face— Taking "a side"
	1	Hardening	I focus on my issues only—I harden my points of view

© *Copyright Center for Aggression Management.*

destructive and therefore aggressive. On the other hand, I can say "Here are my interests. What are your interests, and let us find some common ground so we can move forward." This is cooperative, *constructive* and therefore assertive and not aggressive. Understanding this difference is very important because, no matter where on the Cognitive Aggression Continuum you happen to be, you can stop your upward motion by making this constructive statement. You and the aggressor will typically start de-escalating.

As we escalate on column 3 let's explore "I will plant a seed of distrust with those in his/her community." Your *community* is made up of those individuals with whom you want to be seen. These are the individuals that you like/love and/or respect; and you want them to like/ love and/or respect you. If someone went to your community and spoke about you by saying: "You know Jane. I don't know if I can still trust her. I don't know why, I just don't feel comfortable around her anymore." I have just planted the *seed of distrust*. This insidious seed will grow like weeds in a garden. Partial truth can be far more detrimental than complete truth and this *seed of distrust* is outright Cognitive Aggression at its fourth level. This kind of behavior is used throughout the workplace. We believe that if more individuals understood that they were being overtly aggressive, they would be less likely to use this behavior.

At the fifth level you come out of hiding to declare publicly that your victim is "an enemy" of the community. At the sixth level you make your declaration directly to the victim through an ultimatum. At the seventh level you will demonstrate the potential of your wrath. You will notice that you are not yet using physical force. In Table 2.1 look up the first column to see that you're still in the *escalation phase*, that you have not yet crossed over into the *crisis phase*. Remember we said that typically aggressors do not want to get into a fist fight, because this would mean blood, torn clothing and broken expensive watches. What they are trying to do is to intimidate their opponent into *submission*. By the aggressor demonstrating the potential of his wrath, he is attempting to cause the victim to submit to his control prior to getting into a physical altercation.

As we move into the eighth level we see ourselves in a win/lose situation. We want to win and want our victim to lose. It's that simple.

Finally we come to the ninth level and *Plunging Together into the Abyss*. Here you want to win at any cost, possibly including suicide.

Table 2.3.   Identifying Aggression in Others *and* Threshold to Next Level

Phase	No.	Stage	Identifying Aggression in Others	Threshold to Next Level
Crisis Phase	9	Plunging Together into the Abyss	The Aggressor takes self-destructive action in an attempt to destroy the enemy	Omega
	8	Win/Lose Attack	The Aggressor makes vicious attacks to the enemy's vital areas	Aggressor gives up self-preservation
Escalation Phase	7	Limited Destructive Blows	The Aggressor makes declarations and threats which are followed by interrupted communication—complete detachment occurs	Aggressor prepares to attack the enemy's core
	6	Threat Strategies	The Aggressor presents the ultimatum—he aggressively responds to perceived threats, possibly, on the verge of panic	Aggressor triangulates sanctioned attacks—Aggressor executes ultimatum—righteous indignation
	5	Forced Loss of Face	The Aggressor unmasks his victim as an enemy	Aggressor prepares ultimatum
	4	Image Destruction—Triangulation	The Aggressor demonstrates *deniable punishment behavior,* issues become bipolar, he attacks the victim's core identities	Aggressor prepares to create loss of face
	3	Communicate with Actions vs. Words	The Aggressor takes action without consulting others—the Aggressor appears detached and self absorbed	Aggressor begins attacking victim's image
	2	Debate	The Aggressor becomes fixated on his view, competitive and distrustful	Aggressor takes action without consulting others
	1	Hardening	The Aggressor becomes more distant, argumentative, lacking understanding & empathy	Aggressor begins to position for winning vs. expressing interests and having a winning rational

That's right. We find that all too often suicides are directed at someone else. "I'm really going to get back at my parents by killing myself!" Or, God forbid, it becomes a murder/suicide! Remember the way we identify whether we are being aggressive is through our intent. What is the intent of our action?

Now that we have demonstrated the Nature of Aggression, how can we be better prepared when aggression comes our way?

The final two columns of Table 2.1 allow us to witness aggressive behavior in others and to identify whether aggression is static or escalating. As we discuss the fourth level of aggression under "Identifying Aggression in Others," notice "The Aggressor demonstrates *deniable punishment behavior.*" This is where an aggressor punishes his victim with sarcasm so that later he can say that he was just kidding. This is the action of a "Sniper," which we will discuss in detail later.

CHAPTER 3

The Arts of Aggression Management
Being Prepared

In this chapter we will study the preparation for aggression. We will show how you, as an Aggression Manager, can develop a plan to deal with aggression, institute that plan in your organization and practice its implementation. (By the way, this plan can be applied to household organizations too.) Then, if and when aggression erupts, you can be knowledgeable, trained and practiced to manage aggression effectively and professionally. Plans can include code words and signals through which Aggression Management team members can communicate intentions when aggression reaches its Crisis Phase. As the old saying goes: "if you fail to plan, plan to fail."

In chapter 2, we discussed the fact that in our workplace, our schools and in our society, a lot of people are simply reacting to the problem of aggression. If all you're going to do is *react* to aggression, eventually you will face violence. On this predicate we have built the methodologies of Aggression Management. It is no longer enough to be just *reactive* to aggression. You must *prevent*. This book teaches you how to *prevent* aggression and thereby prevent violence.

There are some traditional initiatives that employers, managers and administrators must consider, beginning with hiring practices. Given the probability and severity of aggression, employers and managers should institute policies and procedures to minimize the risk of employing a potential aggressor. Although we live in a complex, litigious and often angry world, in which it becomes more and more difficult to avoid aggression and violence, an employer can take many steps:

- pre-employment background/work history investigation
- pre-employment drug testing

- posted rules of unacceptable behavior
- random drug testing
- a threat reporting system, including an anonymous tip line
- a threat-of-violence notification system
- a strict policy of zero tolerance for workplace aggression

But even all these steps are not enough. This is a human-based problem and unless you employ human-based skills to solve it, your chances of preventing aggression are slim.

The most important preventative steps for aggression in the workplace are first, evaluation, and second, communication. Every individual should be trained to identify mounting anxiety (defined as anxiety that occurs when an individual feels threatened and stops coping, which begins escalating its way up the Aggression Continuum. Anxiety differs from *fear*, which is a reaction to an actual threat or danger, *anxiety* is a reaction to a perceived threat or danger.) Managers and supervisors should stay in contact with people under their supervision so that they know when factors at work, or outside of work, are becoming potential triggers. The manager who says, "What my employees do after five doesn't concern me," is most likely to be surprised when a sudden act of aggression occurs.

IDENTIFYING AND MANAGING THE UNMAGNIFICENT SEVEN

Adapted from Robert Bramson's *Coping with Difficult People*, we have identified seven basic types of troublesome and potentially aggressive personalities. We call them the Unmagnificent Seven. Each of us may, from time to time, exhibit one or more of these traits, but this is not what we are looking for. We want to focus on those individuals whose Unmagnificent personalities permeate their being, and who use those traits *habitually* as tools to control and manipulate others who work and live around them. Some of these Unmagnificent behaviors can become overtly aggressive, while others can lead to aggressive behavior. Don't assume that someone who exhibits a particular behavior is an aggressor ready to strike. Your challenge is to identify these individuals as one or more of the Unmagnificent Personalities, engage and diffuse their behaviors before they trigger a violent incident.

The Unmagnificent Seven are:

Sherman Tank—Enjoys confrontation; needs to prove himself right; often uses his physical presence, persona or personality to intimidate others.

Sniper—Undermines your authority and morale with criticism behind your back; often uses jokes and sarcasm to cover his sniping. This way he can say "I was just kidding." This is also referred to as Deniable Punishment Behavior, as illustrated in the Cognitive Aggression Continuum, Table 2.1, in which an aggressor can use sniping as a means to punish another and still give them the ability to deny it later.

Exploder—Exhibits mood swings between calm and loud, temperamental outbursts; full of insults and name-calling. The Exploder's goal is to silence the opposition and cow others into submitting to his will.

Complainer—Whines constantly, and feels totally unappreciated and powerless to improve his condition.

Negativist—Says no to every suggestion and is never happy. The Negativist wants everyone to be as miserable as he is. You may

Figure 3.1   Sherman Tank (Created by or for Dr. John D. Byrnes)

Figure 3.2 *Sniper (Created by or for Dr. John D. Byrnes)*

Figure 3.3   *Exploder (Created by or for Dr. John D. Byrnes)*

have heard the statement "Misery loves company." This is not completely true. More accurate is, "Misery loves *miserable* company."

Clam—Remains silent and unresponsive to any request for ideas, suggestions and solutions. Because the Clam keeps his feelings and emotions pent up, he can be the most dangerous of all the Unmagnificent personalities.

Bulldozer—Tries to overwhelm you with facts and figures. His goal is to establish himself as the indispensable expert in everything. The Bulldozer, arrogant and superior in demeanor, has little regard for the knowledge and opinions of others.

DEFUSING THE UNMAGNIFICENT PERSONALITIES

There are five *universal approaches* you can use when dealing with Unmagnificent personalities. For the sake of these illustrations, we'll

Figure 3.4 *Complainer (Created by or for Dr. John D. Byrnes)*

presume that this individual will remain a co-worker, a fellow student or a family member, so you need to continue your relationship with this person. That is why, in part, we want this encounter to be constructive in tone, and not punitive, where the objective would be to apply blame and punishment. These *universal approaches* are meant to be a template only, a guide to assist you in selecting the right words for a particular individual, in a particular environment. The Five Universal Approaches are:

Separate—Separate the Unmagnificent person from his admirers. You either remove him from the crowd or you remove the crowd from him. You may find the latter easier. Does this mean getting the Unmagnificent person alone? Not necessarily. You may need an observer, an advocate or even a professional counselor.

Figure 3.5 *Negativist (Created by or for Dr. John D. Byrnes)*

Compliment—You want this encounter to be constructive, so start
with something positive, i.e., "You are a valued employee, and
you have great talent and ability." You decide what to say based
on the individual and the circumstances surrounding the situation.

Document—Acknowledge the Unmagnificent person for his spe-

Figure 3.6   *Clam (Created by or for Dr. John D. Byrnes)*

cific personality type by documenting and discussing previous
incidents, but doing so in a neutral and constructive manner. We
recommend that prior incidents be documented in writing. It is
imperative that you review them in a calm and neutral way so as
not to incite your aggressor. Behavioral scientists tell us that 7%
of social communication is verbal and 93% is voice tone and body
language. While you can present your evidence verbally with
objectivity, it is far more difficult to portray neutrality. That is
why we suggest written documentation, which may come in useful in the event this action is reviewed by superiors, or even results
in court action.

Convince—Your challenge is to convince this Unmagnificent person
that his behavior is not in his own best interest. This puts him on
notice that he is damaging his case, and indeed his own future
with his behavior, and needs to re-examine his actions immediately. We call this "Impressment," and we'll discuss it in detail
later.

Team Productivity—Finally, you ask the Unmagnificent person,
"How can we work together as a team to be more productive?"

Figure 3.7   *Bulldozer (Created by or for Dr. John D. Byrnes)*

This fifth element is essential because it ties everything else together. It says that you care and respect this person enough to help him work through this process resulting in better productivity for all involved.

A more specific approach can also be used with each of the Unmagnificent personality types. Usually, the Unmagnificent person uses these personality traits as tools, as a means to an end. In addition to the Five Universal Approaches, here are some suggestions to follow when speaking to specific Unmagnificent personality types. Remember, this conversation is held away from the aggressor's crowd.

Sherman Tank—This individual likes everyone to see how intimidating he is. Don't try to out-yell or out-bully this individual. Speak with calm, quiet assurance. If you raise the bar of aggression, he will raise it higher! The result can easily become violent.

Sniper—Be direct. Remembering the third of the Five Universal Approaches, you have documented and can therefore share evidence of his verbal sniping. Try to ascertain what the underlying problem really is. Your exposure of his sniping will make it difficult for him to snipe in the future.

Exploder—This individual also enjoys intimidating. Get him away from his crowd of admirers. Ask him why he has such outbursts of temper. An Exploder will often add weight to his argument by delivering it with emotion (we will discuss emotional weighting in a later chapter). It is important to remain calm and speak with a quiet assurance.

Complainer—Be prepared by documenting his chronic complaints. Convince this compulsive whiner that it would be in his best interests to be more constructive, less of a complainer and to become a team member.

Negativist—Negativism is not based in logic, so never argue the merits of his complaints with this individual. Be aware of what I call the Institutional Negativist. This is a person who is attempting to keep you in a state of fear, often because their job depends upon it. No positive act will dissuade this Negativist from using often-unfounded logic and rationale in an attempt to convince you of your need for their services and/or presence. Often they will weight their rationale with emotions in an attempt to move you away from your logic and rationale toward their emotions so that they can win your confidence. (You will learn more about emotional weighting in chapter 5.) Convince him that it is in his own best interests to exhibit a positive attitude. Keep your statements and outlook positive.

Clam—Begin the discussion yourself, ask questions, then remain silent and listen. Encourage him to open up without seeming to pry. Develop a level of trust. Then you can establish dialogue, identify his behavior and convince the Clam that it is in his best interest to open up and begin contributing as a team member. As we have said, the Clam can be the most dangerous of all the Unmagnificent persons. Since this individual often will not communicate verbally when he is disgruntled, he may "act out" or explode. The Clam is *not* a sleeping dog that you want to leave alone; begin establishing a level of trust and start the communication process as early as possible.

Bulldozer—This type may not be the most dangerous but can be the most difficult. You must silence this individual's continuous chatter so you can begin meaningful communication. Ask this Unmagnificent person a question, any question; then once he has given you an answer, probe that question further. Encourage him to talk until he has nothing left to say—wear him down. Once you have a quiet Bulldozer, you can begin meaningful communication. (As with the other Unmagificents, pursue the idea that, "This behavior is not in your own best interest.")

SEEK THE ADVICE OF A PROFESSIONAL

Some problems run deeper than an Aggression Manager can fathom or handle. If the individual is unaware of his personality trait, refer him to the company's employee assistance program or other psychological assistance program. You must use your best judgment. Consider these characteristics and their severity in the individual:

- Inflexibility
- Hopelessness, an extreme lack of energy
- Identification with perpetrators of violence
- Intimidation of others
- Need to have control over others, manipulative
- Paranoia, views self as a victim of society, family and others
- Socially awkward or uncomfortable
- Difficulty distinguishing between fantasy and reality
- Adverse reaction to constructive criticism
- No responsibility for his own feelings or actions
- Blames others for the consequences of his own actions
- Obsessive dwelling on negativity which produces a worse outcome
- Creates unrest and dissention for the sake of unrest and dissention
- Unreasonable expectations or sense of entitlement ("You owe me . . .")
- History of disciplinary actions

- Obsession with weapons. This is not a strong interest in weapons, but an obsession.
- Identification with or membership in paramilitary organizations
- Police encounters
- Stalking others
- Inability to "let it go," to take no for an answer
- A sentinel event: This is a phrase used in healthcare. It describes the occurrence when an individual responds normally to an abnormal event (such as witnessing a murder) yet considers his response as abnormal and finds himself unable to cope.

TAKING RESPONSIBILITY FOR YOUR ACTIONS

No matter who initiated the aggressive behavior, you will be held responsible for your actions. As an Aggression Manager you must be able to say that you acted judiciously and to the best of your ability, under difficult circumstances, to diffuse the aggressor—and that you take full responsibility for your actions. You may only use "reasonable force" within an aggression moment. The problem is that, what is "reasonable force" may ultimately only be determined in a court of law, not in the aggression moment itself.

Be your own best advocate. In the events that lead up to the aggression moment we often get signs and signals that aggression could occur. When an incident occurs and there are no documented reports or efforts made to deal with this potential, everyone becomes *at risk*. You must be able to state to your company, your school, your parents or the reviewer that: "To the best of my ability, I acted judiciously to remove the possibility of threat." It is therefore in your own best interest to report all threats, veiled or otherwise. You must report any actions, events or statements that you believe will put you or others at risk.

How, for example, would you respond to this example?

Mary told me a few months ago that she had applied for a promotion to a position available in another department. This morning she came out of the supervisor's office looking really upset. She told me a couple of hours later that the manager in the other department had killed her promotion, and "maybe I should kill him." She didn't raise her voice, but I could tell she was angry. She then said that she would make sure that no one in the company would ever again dare to take away a promotion from someone who deserved it. Finally, she suggested that maybe I shouldn't come to work tomorrow morning.

Would you say "it is unusual but it wouldn't concern me?" Would you say "It is strange. I would consider reporting it." Or would you say, "It is threatening and I would report it immediately!" What you decide to do will make a huge difference to the outcome and what effect these circumstances will have on you. Did you act appropriately and professionally under these circumstances? These are some of the questions you'll be asked—and you'd better have very good answers.

Sherry had been having a rough time with her home life. Her husband was arrested for embezzling money from his company. At the same time, Sherry's son joined a gang and developed a drug problem. She seemed depressed and was very upset with her family life. At work her performance began to decline. She became much less personable, and refused to go to the company picnic. Sherry told a friend at the office that she was worried about losing her house, and she would be very mad if she didn't get a big raise. A few days later, Sherry's friend learned that Sherry did not receive the raise and had stormed out of the office.

Once again, how would you respond to these circumstances? Would you say "it is unusual but it wouldn't concern me?" Or, "That's strange. I would consider reporting it?" Or, "It is threatening and I would report it immediately?" Is there a wrong answer? Unless you have a specific policy or procedure that addresses this situation, not really. When do you determine if the way you responded was wrong? When something has gone incredibly wrong and you have not tried to engage the aggressor or documented the aggressor's behavior so that the organization had the opportunity to take action to alleviate the problem.

DOCUMENTATION

In the event of an incident what should you document? Documentation policies differ from organization to organization. Laws regarding the rules of evidence differ from state to state. Check your organization's policy for details and your state's rules on evidence.

- Know what to document—date, day, time, threat made, location, applicable conditions, injuries or property damage. Collect any evidence. Realize that the individual who will review your documentation may possibly make judgments without you present. Because you are an Aggression Manager and therefore have responded in the most effective and professional way possible, we will presume that the demonstrated facts will benefit you. Therefore, it is in your best interest to draw a picture for reviewers that helps take them through the steps that brought you to the conclusion that drove your trained and knowledgeable response.
- Interview all witnesses—Don't miss anyone. Realize that these incidents can result in lawsuits that can generate millions of dollars in liability. Therefore someone is going to be paid thousands of dollars to find fault with your documentation. Nothing against you personally. They just want a win that will result in a potentially large reward for them. If you have missed a witness, especially a counter-opinioned witness, do you think they will find this witness? You bet they will! And your documentation and credibility will suffer for it. Be aware that when a witness sees an unfamiliar shape or scene, they often automatically correct it to some more familiar schema. As a result, witnesses will often think that they see something familiar when in fact they don't. Your challenge is to expose the witness to what actually occurred in a way that they can accept as truth.
- Avoid delay—Act while memories are fresh. Delay can cause distortions. Be aware that your adrenaline rush can also create distortions.
  - *Tachypsychia*, a distortion that occurs when your mind speeds up to cope with an aggressive moment and it causes our perception of that event to seem as though it were in slow motion.
  - *Tunnel Vision,* our peripheral vision reduces down to transfix on a threatening focal point.
  - *Auditory Exclusion,* the loss of hearing due to the adrenaline rush. Law enforcement officers have told me that they saw the

gun, they saw the flare as the bullet was ejected through the gun barrel and they saw the window glass break behind them but they never heard the explosion of the bullet.

Your challenge is to see through the effects of the adrenaline rush and help the witnesses do the same.

- Be objective—Not subjective. Just the facts, please, not your opinion. Let those who review your report come to the same opinion that you have by offering the facts in a way that convinces them that you acted professionally.
- Organize chronologically—Recount everything as if writing a script.
- Tell the truth—A single untruth, distortion or exaggeration can undermine your entire documentation. Remember—someone is being paid thousands of dollars to undermine your credibility. These cases go to court, not weeks away, but years away. It is hard enough to remember the truth, much less a lie, two years from now when this case goes to court.

Should you share your documentation with others? First it is important to understand the *rules of evidence*. Each state may approach this a little differently, so check with a local attorney. Generally the rule is: if you document an incident but you share it with no one and tell no one about its existence, that documentation is yours alone. On the other hand, if you document and share it with someone or tell someone else about its existence, then your documentation can be subpoenaed. If you intend to share your documentation with others, as we typically suggest that you do, make sure that it can hold up under cross-examination. We recommend that you share your documentation with the person to whom you report. Why? Because this person may be able to help in a more effective way due to his or her position. Also, you are sharing the risk. You are putting them on notice, should further incidents occur, they too are at risk.

CHAPTER 4

The Art of Persuasion—Part 1

Understanding Aggression's Effects on Communication

In the aggression environment, an Aggression Manager may have only moments to persuade an aggressor from committing a violent act. In chapter 2, we discussed at length the Aggression Continuum, and how to track the mounting anxiety of an emerging aggressor along that continuum—through behavioral signs, physiological changes in the body and the increased use of verbal aggression. The next four chapters deal in depth with the second Art of Aggression Management, the Art of Persuasion, which is comprised of four areas of persuasive skills:

1. Communicating with the aggressor
2. Pacing the aggressor—strategies
3. Pacing the aggressor with verbal techniques
4. Pacing the aggressor with nonverbal techniques, effectively reading and utilizing body language.

This chapter will focus on the process of communication and its related techniques that the Aggression Manager can use to effectively assume and maintain control over an aggressor.

THE COMMUNICATION PROCESS

To start this chapter refer to Figure 4.1, where we see an Aggression Manager, the *sender*, at one end and an Aggressor, the *receiver*, at the other. It is not our purpose here to discuss the casual communication process but rather to explain how aggression affects this process. If you're conducting a casual conversation with a receiver, you would

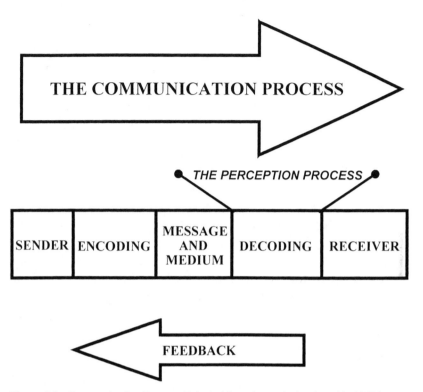

Figure 4.1 *Communication Process (Adapted from the work developed in 1947 by a mathematician named Claude Shannon. Shannon explained the process mathematically with a non-mathematical interpretation by Warren Weaver).*

expect this conversation to be mutual and bilateral. But if you're an Aggression Manager conducting the communication process with an aggressor, you must take 100% responsibility for this process. If you aren't prepared to take total responsibility, get someone who will, because the chances are, you will not be able to work through the maze of filters put up by the aggressor.

As we move through the communication process, the Aggression Manager expresses ideas, emotions and strategies by encoding them into words. She translates (*message*) them both verbally and non-verbally, either face-to-face, over the phone or in memo format (*medium*). Then she comes to the most difficult part of this process, the decoding of her words by the aggressor. This is difficult because it involves the perceptions of the aggressor. It is our challenge to identify these perceptions and, through their understanding, motivate the aggressor away from an aggressive act.

THE PERCEPTION PROCESS

As I trace the *perception process*, you will see the five filters a message goes through before it reaches an aggressor's mind as a complete communication. The strength of these filters determines whether and to what extent an Aggression Manager may be effectively communicating with an individual moving up the Aggression Continuum.

Triggers

Remember the Aggression Continuum (Table 2.1). Persons, events, situations and objects are the stimuli that color the aggressor's perception. A deeply-resented boss, a recent firing, a pressure-charged work

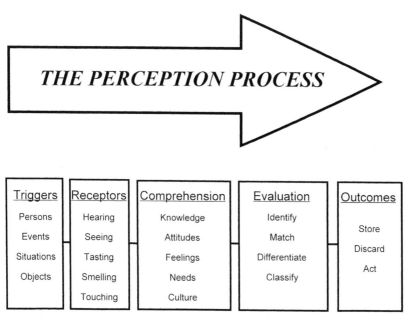

Triggers	Receptors	Comprehension	Evaluation	Outcomes
Persons	Hearing	Knowledge	Identify	Store
Events	Seeing	Attitudes	Match	Discard
Situations	Tasting	Feelings	Differentiate	Act
Objects	Smelling	Needs	Classify	
	Touching	Culture		

Figure 4.2 *Perception Process*

environment or a weapon hidden in a pocket—all these are triggers which may bend and distort an incoming verbal communication. As an Aggression Manager, your challenge is to identify the aggressor's trigger(s) and reconcile them.

Receptors

The five senses—hearing, seeing, touching, smelling and tasting—can also filter or obstruct information. If you have an emerging aggressor who is standing next to noisy equipment or listening to a crowd of admirers, remove him from the area so you can gain his full attention. If you do not have his undivided attention you will diminish your ability to move him away from an aggressive act. You must make a professional judgment. Will you wait until he is completed with what distracts him or will you remove him from this distraction? Either way it is imperative that you have his undivided attention.

Comprehension

The aggressor understands a message within the bounds of his own experience in five areas:

1. Knowledge Base. The Aggression Manager must speak to the knowledge level of the aggressor, not her own, not only to communicate more effectively but not to appear to be condescending to the aggressor.
2. Attitudes. The aggressor harbors attitudes that must be addressed, especially with regard to managers and supervisors, e.g., "You work up there in that ivory tower. What do you know about working on the plant floor?" This also applies to adults and children. Your challenge is to identify these attitudes and work through them; otherwise you may hit a brick wall of communication.
3. Feelings. These include misplaced anger, peer pressure, stress, fear, low self-esteem or any of a number of other issues. Feelings can affect an aggressor's ability to resolve issues. At the same time, they can be quite confounding to us as Aggression Managers because, in most cases, we have not helped create them. Yet

they can have a profound effect on the outcome of an incident. We must identify these feelings and either diminish them or use them to move the aggressor away from an aggressive act.

4. Needs. An aggressor has needs at many levels of his life. Using Abraham Maslow's Hierarchy of Needs, the Aggression Manager must, in a moment, determine at what level of need the aggressor resides, acknowledge it and briefly validate that need, e.g., "You might be right, Joe, I think I understand why you feel that way." Then the Aggression Manager, with respect, eases "Joe" toward his own goals, and works within that context toward resolution.

Do you think people's needs change throughout their lives?

Figure 4.3   *Hierarchy of Needs and Wants (Adapted from Abraham H. Maslow's Hierarchy of Needs,* Eupsychian Management, *a series of his journal notes from the early 1960s.)*

Absolutely. You are flying along at 37,000 feet contemplating the needs of your career and your family when suddenly the plane loses cabin pressure and falls 10,000 feet before the pilot regains control. Suddenly, you may be more immediately concerned with your basic need for survival. Needs can be elusive, both yours and the aggressor's. Your challenge is to identify where the aggressor's *needs* are and then respectfully bring him to where *your* needs are: to resolve his issues without the use of aggression.

5. Culture—Whether the aggressor is from Iran or Iowa, Memphis or Mexico, he is bound by traditions and customs of culture. The successful Aggression Manager must deal knowledgeably in the framework of those customs, and not ignore or belittle them. The subject of cultural diversity focuses on our differences. To be an effective Aggression Manager we must be aware of our differences but we must focus on our similarities. It is our objective to develop trust. Why? The more we develop trust the less we become a threat.

How do we develop trust? Who do *you* trust? You trust people who look like you, talk like you, dress like you and act like you. You trust you!

To develop trust, we must find things in common with the aggressor and build on those commonalities. All of us, regardless of our differences, have many characteristics in common. We all dislike rejection, ridicule and embarrassment. We all seek connection with others, care what others think about us and enjoy recognition and attention. We all seek to establish a degree of control over our lives, and will do more to avoid pain than we will to seek pleasure. The Aggression Manager who protests, "I have nothing in common with him" simply hasn't looked upon the aggressor as another human being and needs to try harder. The more we develop trust, the less we are seen by the aggressor as a threat. Resolution is nearly impossible without this trust. So the more that is established in common, the quicker the essential element of trust is created between the aggressor and the Aggression Manager. As an aside, one way to convince an aggressor that you can be trusted is to appear to be acting against your own self-interest.

Proxemics as an Element of Culture

Proxemics is a term for the distance one person likes to maintain between himself and another person. The power of proxemics is wonderfully illustrated in an exercise we conduct in our workshops.

We start by positioning half the class against a wall on one side of the room facing out, and the other half facing them at about five feet apart. We ask them to partner with each other and we number the half against the wall "Ones" and the other half "Twos."

We start with twos moving at a slow pace toward ones, with the Instruction to ones that when twos get "close enough" raise your hand and twos will stop immediately. When all twos have stopped, we observe that the line made by the approaching twos is not straight, illustrating that each human prefers a different distance. None of the distances established are wrong, just different.

Because turnabout is fair play, we now have the Ones approach the Twos and we learn an important lesson: your own partner may not let you get as close as you would let him or her get. Why is that important? When you find yourself in front of an aggressor, you might approach that aggressor to a distance at which you would be comfortable. Sud-

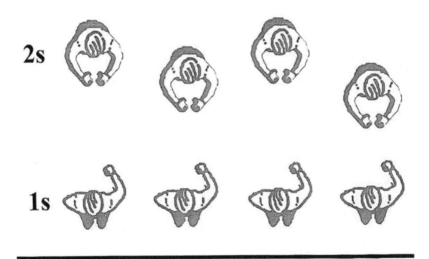

Figure 4.4 *Proximics Exercise (Created by or for Dr. John D. Byrnes)*

denly the aggressor begins escalating. Although the distance is all right for you, it is not all right with the aggressor.

Finally we ask the Ones, who now stand inches away from the Twos, to turn their bodies at a 45-degree angle toward their partner. We call this "Blading." Keeping eye contact with their partner, we now ask them to continue to approach their partner and typically they are able to reduce the distance by half. This too is an important lesson. We learn that when you Blade the aggressor it offers you the ability to get closer to the aggressor without causing him to escalate, a valuable tool for an Aggression Manager approaching an aggressor.

Americans typically like three feet of distance when standing face-to-face, a foot-and-a-half to their side and five feet to their back. Do you remember, when you were younger, ever walking along a darkening road at dusk? Suddenly someone you didn't know walked up from behind. Remember how uncomfortable, even frightened that made you? An aggressor may be treading in his own darkness, so be very careful walking up to him from behind.

Why do people require these distances? There are many influences: age, gender, size, hygiene, culture, familiarity, environment, background, etc., But this can be something as subtle as coming from a family of huggers, or coming from the country versus coming from the city.

2s

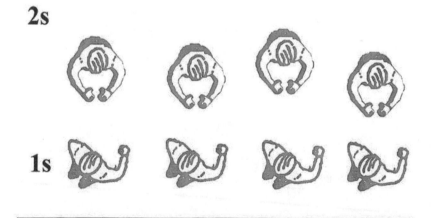

1s

Figure 4.5 *Proximics Blading Exercise (Created by or for Dr. John D. Byrnes)*

How do we know when we are getting too close to an aggressor? Because they step back! Or the aggressor puts an object, like a chair, between you and him. Or he may cross his arms, symbolically covering up his *lifeline*.

Cultural Prejudice

Finally, the greatest obstacle to the resolution of aggression with regard to culture is prejudice. In other words, we prejudge. It is important to note that if you are human, you will prejudge. It is part of the human condition. Sociologists call this attitude "ethnocentrism," the natural tendency to consider our nation, our race, our geographical area superior to everyone else's. It's what I call the "us and them" syndrome. This syndrome is often something as simple as "us" is our favorite football team and "them" is the other team. Or it can be an attitude as destructive as plain bigotry.

We have already said that the best way to bring you and an aggressor together is through a process of identifying and developing those things that you and the aggressor have in common, thereby developing trust. So what more divisive action can you take than to wallow in and continue to focus on those things that make you different. The rule is simple: focus on similarities—bring people together, focus on differences—push people apart. Our challenge as Aggression Managers is to intellectualize beyond our prejudices. Any prejudice on our part will diminish our ability to persuade an aggressor away from an aggressive act. So we must push beyond those prejudices—beginning immediately.

Evaluation

The aggressor applies what you are communicating to himself. Without this personal application, the aggressor won't be motivated to do what you want him to do. How do you determine whether he is evaluating what you say? You ask him, not in a condescending way, but with respect: "Sometimes I have difficulty expressing myself. Please help me out. Could you tell me, just in your own words, what we've been talking about." If the aggressor is indeed evaluating, you'll hear a replay in his own words what and how you have communicated. This is important because you'll identify whether you need to restate or clarify anything you've already said.

Outcome

Finally you come to the point where you determine whether the aggressor will discard, store or act on what you've told him. You, of course, want the aggressor to act on the strength of your persuasion. Otherwise the aggressor may react violently.

It is essential to an Aggression Manager to effectively understand the communication process in the aggressive environment. Even with an inventory of other verbal persuasion skills, without understanding how to communicate effectively within the context of aggression, you may simply be saying nice things that have little or no effect on the aggressor.

CHAPTER 5

The Art of Persuasion—Part 2

Pacing the Aggressor—Strategies

As I previously indicated, the Arts of Aggression Management are threefold: the Art of Being Prepared, the Art of Persuasion and the Art of Safe Escape. In chapter 2, I discussed at length the Aggression Continuum, and how to track the mounting anxiety of an emerging aggressor along that continuum—through behavioral signs, physiological changes in the body and the increased use of verbal aggression and the Verbal Aggression Scale.

As part of becoming prepared to deal with aggression, I identified the Unmagnificent Seven types of troublesome personalities, and showed how best to deal with them. Every Aggression Manager must anticipate that the time will come when he faces an aggressor, and will be expected to use his training to take the initiative in mitigating or defusing aggression. In fact, beyond simply anticipating an aggressive situation, the Aggression Manager should have already made the commitment to become involved, to have a plan and to take responsibility for whatever actions are required.

But regardless of all the planning and preparation and textbook knowledge, Aggression Management strategies and even tactical rehearsals are no substitute for suddenly being thrust into *the real thing*.

The next three chapters deal in depth with Pacing the Aggressor, the art of convincing someone to agree with you, because they believe it is good for them; the strategies of Pacing the Aggressor with verbal and nonverbal techniques; and the effective use and reading of body language.

Persuasion is not necessarily a gentle art, although it is best practiced as such at the outset of an aggressive incident. Many aggressors can indeed be artfully nudged out of their aggressive intent, while some require stronger persuasion. I like to characterize Pacing the Aggressor as a "coming alongside" an aggressor, and then using the many persuasive Pacing the Aggressor skills to induce that individual to think your way—while he is buying into the notion that it was *his own* idea.

AUTOCRATIC VERSUS CONVINCING

One of the most profound discoveries I made as I explored Aggression Management was autocratic persuasion versus convincing. It has always been understood that persuasion was made up of two basic approaches: autocratic and democratic.

Autocratic persuasion means the use of an authoritarian or militarist manner. "Be here at 8:00 A.M. tomorrow morning." "Just say No!" "Just do it!" Democratic persuasion gives someone the opportunity and time to make their own decision. If you are an Aggression Manager and your challenge is to persuade an aggressor away from an act of aggression, you do not have the luxury of allowing that aggressor to make up his own mind. He may choose an act of aggression. You must convince him that your suggestions are in his best interest.

So I changed our illustration to be autocratic persuasion versus convincing. Webster's defines *convincing* as, "to persuade by argument or proof, or cause to believe in." In our case, convincing means causing the aggressor to go where you want him to go and have him believe that it is his idea. How do you accomplish this? You must demonstrate that your ideas for him are in his best interest by identifying those things that move him and push those buttons to motivate him in your direction. How? That's what this book is all about.

CONVINCE RATHER THAN DEMAND

I have taken this concept to employers, explaining that if they would invest the time to convince their employees rather than making autocratic demands, these employees would buy into their requests, and become self-motivated to accomplish their goals. Employers would not need to supervise and manage as closely; employees would become more productive; and the company would become more productive and profitable.

I have taken this to schools, explaining that if teachers would invest the time to convince the students that understanding this knowledge was in their best interest rather than teaching, as some do, in a more pedantic way, students would buy into the need for learning and would be self-motivated to learn and apply their education. Students would require less rote learning and supervision. Students who are involved in their learning are less aggressive. The learning environment between teacher and student would vastly improve and students would get higher achievement scores.

I have even taken this to the military. I know the military is an autocratic culture. But many military personnel manage and supervise civilian employees. Military hospitals, administrative and support services, shipyards and other bases and activities are often administered by military personnel but are staffed primarily by a civilian work force. Supposing an officer or Master Sergeant command a civilian worker to perform a task, and the civilian worker responds "I can't do that. It's against my union contract." Where can the military supervisor go? He can employ the art of convincing! It works.

THE UMBRELLA OF TRUST

Before you can successfully deploy any strategy or tactic of persuasion in an aggressive situation, you must build trust. It is the big umbrella under which you must perform your repertoire of persuasive skills and talents.

Suppose for a moment you've received a call from your boss that Bruto, the big guy down at the loading dock, has his supervisor cornered and is threatening to cleave his skull with a tire iron. Since you have a certificate stating that you're an Aggression Manager, everyone follows you down to the dock to see how you're going to handle Bruto, who stands 6'4" and weighs 260 pounds.

When you arrive, a noisy crowd has gathered, and bets are already being made as to the outcome. Bruto is angry, threatening, loud and profane—but the supervisor's head is still intact. He can tell at a glance that

1. you are a threat, because you've come to dissuade him from doing something he's already promised to do;
2. you are obviously a "suit" from an air-conditioned office who knows nothing about the dock;
3. you have no idea or even care why he's had to resort to pounding his supervisor with a tire iron.

Remember: trust is not instinctual. It must be earned. Your first task is to begin building a bridge of trust with an individual with whom it would appear, at first glance, you have absolutely nothing in common. Bridge building begins with your search for things that you and Bruto have in common, so you can start creating a climate of trust on those fragments of commonality.

Another trust builder is *empathy*. The word itself derives from *em* in Latin, a prefix that means, "put one's self into," and *pathy* from the Greek for "suffering" or "feeling." You must demonstrate empathy to the plight or perceived injustices suffered by the aggressor. In the next chapter, we show how the technique of paraphrasing conveys your empathy.

Since "threat" and "trust" are at opposing ends of the spectrum, the more trust you develop, the less of a threat you are. The underlying question is, "Who do we trust?" We innately trust someone who talks like we talk, thinks like we think, dresses like we dress. We trust *us*! Since few of us are so conveniently alike in these respects, when trust must be quickly cobbled together, we have to seek other, not so obvious similarities. Probe for hometowns or home states, kids, similar tastes, interests or life experiences.

"Yeah, I was in 'Nam too, First Cav, Third Division . . ."

"Sure, I've got a daughter that age. That's a tough age, isn't it?"

"Ohio? I grew up north of Dayton."

Even more basic, most of us have things in common because we're human beings:

- We seek connection with others.
- We're saddened by loss and try to avoid it.
- We don't like rejection.
- We like recognition and attention.

- We will do more to avoid pain than we will to seek pleasure.
- We dislike ridicule and embarrassment.
- We care what others think of us.
- We seek a degree of control over our lives.
- We need a degree of dignity.

If you turn to an emerging aggressor and say "it really upset me when someone ridicules and embarrasses me in front of my friends, too." What have you just done? I have instantly created the beginnings of rapport and you are on your way to trust.

You and Bruto have a good deal in common after all. So you engage him in conversation, get him talking about himself, his family, what he values in his life. You demonstrate genuine, natural interest, without a hint of patronizing him. In all likelihood, you may be the first person to listen to the guy for a long time. The more he talks, the more he will come to trust you as an objective individual who can get him out of a bad situation; and the less likely he will be to crack the supervisor's head.

SOLUTIONPERSON

In my seminars around the country, I tell the story of the top business executive I knew years ago. I asked him once what accounted for his success in dealing with so many challenges day after day. He smiled and told me that if he were to open up his shirt, I would see a big "S" on his chest, and it stood for "Solutionman." His philosophy was to seek solutions, whatever that took—not assign blame, nor take sides, nor make excuses, nor sit around complaining, but to solve problems. He repeated the old saying with new vigor, "If you're not part of the solution, you're part of the problem."

I've thought about that over the years, and adopted his philosophy in my own career. Part of gaining trust is being perceived as one who seeks solutions. If you refuse to become part of the problem and only permit yourself to be part of the solution, more than likely you will say and do the right things to become what I now refer to, in deference to the men *and* women in my audiences, as "Solutionperson."

But what do you do? How do you "pull alongside" the aggressor and deftly position yourself to lead him away from a possible act of violence? You do so by identifying the values that motivate this aggressor; then you respectfully persuade him in the direction you want him to go.

WHAT THE AGGRESSOR VALUES

Most individuals place a high priority in one or more element of their lives. As we probe for these high priority values, we know they fall into five categories:

The Value of Time

Time is a precious commodity. In our culture, we think of time as a sort of currency that we "spend," "invest," or "waste." We say, "time is money," and "time is precious." Part of its value is that we have a limited amount of it, and become impatient about using what we do have unwisely. Ask the aggressor if he has thought about how much time he is going to lose if he goes through with his threat or doesn't end the incident he has begun. The ultimate loss of time, of course, is months or even years in prison. You need to emphasize this possibility up front. At the very least, he may have to spend hours talking to lawyers and law enforcement officials, looking for another job or just waiting to hear the outcome of his actions. *"Bruto, have you got time for all the hassle you may be creating? You're going to be wasting a lot of time, and if you're like me you don't have a lot of time in your day to waste. But it's up to you."*

The Value of Money

Even if he feels he is justified in his actions, the aggressor faces attorney's fees, investigation costs and other expenses he can't even anticipate and certainly can't afford. At the same time, he may lose his source of income, and have a difficult time finding another job that pays enough to meet his living expenses. *"Bruto, how are you going to support your family if you lose this job? What about payments on that truck you bought last month? And, of course, you'd lose your medical insurance. Is this worth losing all that?"*

The Value of Job

Almost everyone who has a job enjoys the prestige of having that job, and has also felt the anxiety of not having one. A job contributes not only income and a sense of self-worth, but security and peace of mind. A job with some problems is better than no job. *"Bruto, you've got a good job here. How long would it take to find another one that pays this well?"*

The Value of Record

Beyond the job itself, most individuals place a high value on the record they've achieved. For many, the stress of continuing high performance, or frustration and anger at not being recognized for that record of performance, is what pushes them toward aggression. Appeal to their pride in their record, and to their sense of professionalism, which is a genuine source of dignity. *"Bruto, you've been here for 15 years. You've got an excellent record, and even if you don't think you've been treated fairly, you don't want to spoil that record with one incident like this."*

There is a dark side to one's record to consider as well—a *criminal* record. You may recall that in chapter 1 a survey from the Society for Human Resources Management (SHRM) found only 2% of aggressors have a criminal record. So for the vast majority of aggressors, the possibility of a criminal record would certainly be significant incentive to end the incident.

The Value of Family

Few individuals want to let their families down. Love and loyalty are strong values regardless of the makeup of the household. Few are indifferent about "letting the kids down" or putting the family in financial jeopardy. *"Bruto, what's your wife going to think? What about your daughter. She really looks up to you."*

Ask questions, that help you ascertain which values the aggressor holds in highest priority, then show him how his actions are threatening those values. Because you don't really know which of these values, or which combination, is likely to impact the aggressor's thinking, you need to wrap them all up into one summation of possibilities. *"Bruto, if you really tried to hurt Johnson, or actually hurt him, the law might see it as assault, or even attempted murder. You'd have a criminal record. We'd have no choice. You'd lose your job and your health insurance. What would your wife and daughter think then? How would you be seen by your friends and co-workers, as a fair-minded guy?"*

USING DEFENSIVE STRATEGIES

When you arrive at the scene of an incident to begin your intervention, the aggressor is no doubt in a dark and uncooperative mood. He is not just waiting for you to suggest this or that, so he can disarm himself emotionally and return to his job. He's likely to be belligerent and confrontational.

So as you begin to lay out your strategies in your mind, searching for the crux of the matter, building trust and asking questions, the aggressor may begin some form of verbal counterattack. This is most likely to occur if you're starting to make sense, "winning" the conversation with logic that may imply to the aggressor that he is illogical. Whereas you're using the constructive techniques of verbal persuasion to move a person away from an act of aggression toward some resolution, he may use manipulation to try to control and obstruct you, in order to win a personal victory. The difference between your persuasion and his manipulation is intent.

Emotional Weighting

One counter-strategy he may use is emotional weighting. The aggressor will begin to weight the discussion with emotion. His face may redden with anger; he may become intimidating and even threatening. Alternatively he may weaken and become teary eyed. What is the aggressor's objective? If he can succeed in spiking your emotions, getting you to yell back, causing you to move from your logic and reason to his emotions then he wins! But you can control the impact of an aggressor's emotional weighting.

What is your defense? To begin with, maintain your calm. Calm, like anger, panic or any other emotion, is contagious. And just as one person's anger feeds off another's to grow in intensity, a calm demeanor throws water on that growing rage by not responding to it.

Right-Brain versus Left-Brain Thinking

You must also apply the subtle skills of moving the aggressor from his emotional right-brain faculties to his analytical left-brain faculties. You may already be aware of right and left brain functions. We know that the right brain processes such activities as imagination, color, music, rhythm, daydreaming, creating pictures in our head, our sensitivity and our emotions; the left brain processes such activities as mathematics (numerological), linear thinking, language, logic, writing and anything analytical. Although it may seem that some people you know lack a right or left brain, we know that everyone has both. In fact, you can move someone from one side of their brain to the other by simply activating that side of the brain. By asking a question that requires left brain action you can move someone away from their emotions (crying, anger, aggression) into an analytical process. Ask them to write down, in detail, what they have experienced. Ask them what skills they have used in the past to deal with emotionally charged issues. Start counting off numbered ways that you can resolve the aggressor's problems. An example of this is when we feel ourselves getting angry, we might tell ourselves to count to ten. We respond to an aggressor with "Here is what I can do to help you. First I will . . . Second I will . . . Third I will . . ." As the aggressor follows your list; the act of mentally tabulating tempers the emotional impact of right-brain thinking. Each of these ideas move the aggressor from their right-brain emotions to left-brain analytical thinking, helping them to regain their quality of judgment and moving them toward a resolution that is nonaggressive.

Objective versus Subjective Perspective

Civilization is built on absolutes. An absolute is an objective and universal truth accepted by everyone, or at least the majority, to judge "right" from "wrong," "good" from "bad," "acceptable behavior" from "unacceptable behavior." *"Thou shalt not kill,"* springs to mind.

By contrast, chaos is created by relatives. I don't mean visiting cousins, but by subjective rules of behavior set independently by each individual. The sixties mantra, *"If it feels good, do it,"* comes to mind. Standards of law and order are undermined in a society where absolute and objective rules are replaced by relative and subjective ones.

People need "objective perspective" as opposed to a "subjective perspective." Let's take, for example, the subjective word "fairness." Fairness for one person can be in complete opposition to another person. Two individuals, completely justified by their "fairness," could be in complete conflict with each other, sometimes to the point of war. Once upon a time, early communities decided that, for its members to live peacefully with one another, there had to be objective rules that everyone had to abide by. These rules are often referred to as the "rule of law." No single rule or law can apply to all people, all the time, so the application of these rules had to be measured and changed as the need for change arrived. Without an objective view of issues there would be no consensus, no accepted standards for everyone to abide by. Subjective or relative standards would prevail and chaos could rule.

The understanding between subjective and objective perspective is essential to an Aggression Manager. Your challenge is to cause an aggressor, who sees his situation subjectively from his viewpoint, to see things objectively. Aggressors who do not want to obey the rules will rely on a subjective position to justify their actions. Aggressors may insist that the rules are "unfair, uncaring, mean spirited, outdated or irrelevant." Your challenge is to see through this subjective verbiage and, using your professional judgment, bring this individual back to an objective understanding of the issues.

Most people believe that they have an objective perspective but the reality is that virtually every person looks at the world through the window of his or her own perspective, a window clouded by bias, and tinted with a lifetime of personal experiences.

Here's an example (Figure 5.1). Do you see a grotesque old woman? Do you see a fashionable young woman? Or do you see both? A higher truth is at work here. There is neither an old woman nor a young woman. There is only a white background and black lines.

Figure 5.1   *Perception Exercise (Stephen R. Covery,* The 7 Habits of Highly Effective People, Powerful Lessons in Personal Change, *Simon & Schuster, New York, 1990.)*

See how our perspective can mislead us? We must identify what our aggressor's perspective is, to some degree acknowledge their feelings, give them some brief sense of validation and then bring them to our more objective perspective. What is our objective perspective? Our perspective is that the aggressor must resolve his issues without aggression. It is important to note that, although individuals will kill each other and nations will go to war with each other over differences in perspective, perspectives can change in an instant. (In modern history, for example, the Soviet Union was an American ally during World War II in the common cause to destroy Nazism. Virtually the day that war ended, perspectives changed, and the Soviet Union became the cold war foe of the United States. Now 50 years later the Soviet Union's successor, Russia, becomes our ally again to fight terrorism in Afghanistan.) Your challenge is to identify what are the aggressor's motives, their intent, and convince them that your objective perspective is in their best interest. The Aggression Manager must realize that, to this individual, their perspective represents their "truth." Do not reject their truth because in doing so you reject them. Accept their truth and then say "however," or I like "yes, well" followed by persuasion that moves the aggressor away from his aggression. Better yet, say "and," then persuade. The aggressor may follow you and not realize that he has been moved from his "truth."

Motivation

What motivates your aggressor? If you can identify what moves your aggressor, you can push the buttons that direct the aggressor in the direction you wish to go. Sometimes simply the question: "What's your favorite thing to do?" can identify what stimulates your aggressor away from or toward the direction you want. As we consider motivation it is important to note that often humans buy into an idea because of emotions and justify their decision with facts. It is important not to become a victim of your emotions but to use them persuasively to move an aggressor away from an aggressive act. The use of *stories* can be an effective way to tap into an aggressor's emotions.

Away from versus toward Something

Most people, depending upon circumstances, are motivated either *toward something*, in pursuit of a goal or an objective; or *away from something* in an attempt to avoid risk, fear or making a mistake. Is your aggressor motivated away from something? Find out what that something is and you can push the correct buttons to move your aggressor away from an aggressive act.

It might be effective to say, "Let's figure out what's wrong. There's no problem that we can't solve together." With an aggressor who is motivated toward something you might ask, "What do you have to gain if you become aggressive?" or away from something, "What do you have to lose if you become aggressive?" and "We can solve this problem now before it becomes a serious issue in the future." In order to learn whether you're dealing with a "*toward something* individual" or an "*away from something* individual" ask the question: "So that I can better help you, tell me why it's important to you to do this?" Listen to whether they choose an answer the moves them away from something or toward something. What are some of the things that we are motivated away from: criticism, loss of our possessions, pain, loss of reputation, loss of money, trouble. Or, we are motivated toward: achieving the freedom of our time, more money, the prestige that goes with our job or a job opportunity, our health, maintain or enhance our reputation, achieve the respect of our loved ones, experience pleasure, gratify our curiosity, attract someone of the opposite sex or to take advantage of an opportunity.

Internally versus Externally Thinking

Most humans, again depending on circumstances, are motivated either through an *internal thinking* process or an *external thinking* process—by internal measurements or by external influences. They either measure how they will respond to your input internally, through a process of looking within themselves and analyzing the input based on their own internal standards; or they will respond to your input externally, through the facts, figures and information delivered by you or others.

An internally motivated individual does not readily respond to demands. You must convince an internally motivated person that the direction you wish him to go is in his best interest. He will take an autocratic suggestion simply as information, process it and make what he believes to be an appropriate judgment from it. Internally motivated individuals tend to think others are wrong when they disagree with them. You may hear them say: "That person is a jerk because he doesn't appreciate what I have done for him."

Externally motivated individuals are influenced greatly by your advice and what they perceive as the opinions and wishes of those whom they respect. You may be more autocratic with an externally motivated aggressor but remember being autocratic is like having anchovies on your pizza—a little goes a long way.

With an internally motivated aggressor you may want to offer input as options for them to consider. You can ask them "When do you know that you're anxious?" and "Where do you feel this anxiety?" Internally motivated aggressors will often point to where on their bodies' they feel their anxiety. An externally motivated aggressor will probably have no idea what you're talking about. It is important to note that the context of the circumstances can change someone from an externally to internally motivated person. An individual may be internally motivated in most business situations, but when placed under the anxiety of aggression, he may look for guidance from those around him, externally.

Global versus Linear Thinkers

Most people are motivated through either global thinking or linear thinking. Global thinkers see the big picture. They can follow a linear presentation of specific details but get bored very quickly. To persuade this aggressor, you need to present the big picture, the main idea, the macro view instead of getting bogged down in details and specifics. You can identify this aggressor because he may express himself in vague subjective terms, leaving out important details. Your challenge is to help this aggressor communicate more objectively. This objectivity, if applied thoughtfully, can trigger the analytical left brain and help move the aggressor away from their emotional right brain.

The linear thinker loves the details and seldom becomes bored with the specifics. More extreme linear thinkers may have difficulty grasping the bigger picture. It may be more effective to communicate your position in a more sequential way. Start at the beginning and make each step precise and detailed. Make sure he grasps each step before going to the next step.

Status Quo versus Change Thinkers

Most individuals are also motivated through either a desire to maintain constancy—the status quo—or through the excitement of change. In fact, change is the only constant we can count on! Change always upsets the individual who wants things as they've always been. Because he resists change, it's hard to persuade this aggressor with words like "new," "different" and "revolutionary." He needs reassurance that change will not endanger that with which he is so comfortable—starting with his job! It's better to explain how the path of change is not so different than what he's used to, with some advantages that will help him, make his job easier and make his future more secure. Also reassure him that he can count on you to be there to help with this process.

Change-oriented individuals, on the other hand, look forward to and embrace change. You can persuade this aggressor with words like "new," "different" and "revolutionary." Offer this advocate of change the opportunity of an adventure. Point out that he is the only person who can resolve this issue, and describe him as uniquely qualified and capable. *"Bruto, you've got the intellect and skills to help us solve this problem like no one else I can think of."*

Non-Plus

"Non-plus" is a term used by my late mother to describe being perceived as contributing no emotional input to a situation or issue; in other words, appearing completely neutral. In most circumstances, you as an Aggression Manager will be more affective when you don't add any of your emotion to a situation unless, of course, you're using emotion as a tool. This does not mean for a moment that you are not a catalyst to what will occur next. Quite the contrary, you will quietly observe the aggressor's strengths and weaknesses and push the right buttons to move the aggressor in the direction that you wish them to move—away from an aggressive act.

Strengths versus Weaknesses

As an Aggression Manager you will need to observe and respond effectively to an aggressor's strengths and weaknesses. This will, of course, require your effective use of non-plus behavior. If, as an example, an aggressor uses sniping, cutting or insulting behavior, he is likely feeling threatened. He may feel insecure about his inability to handle day-to-day challenges, or to relate to others around him.

Because people want a degree of control over their environment, they'll sometimes put up a facade to protect themselves from having to deal with those around them. Often they believe that, if they sting you with their rapier wit, they'll disarm your ability to challenge them on more meaningful issues. This behavior masks weakness and needs to be dealt with head on. Use an Unmagnificent Seven universal approach for a Sniper, and try to eliminate such behavior.

Least Possible Applause

As an Aggression Manager, you may be called upon to discourage an aggressor's behavior in the most subtle and unobtrusive way. I remember observing experts training dolphins, and watched them use a technique called Least Possible Applause (LPA). When a dolphin performed correctly they would applaud vigorously and reward the animal. When a dolphin performed incorrectly, they used LPA. They would stand still and expressionless, demonstrating their disapproval of unacceptable performance. It worked with dolphins. I feel that the principal of LPA, showing disapproval by demonstrating no reaction at all to unacceptable behavior, is effective in instances where an aggressor is seeking reaction to gauge his effectiveness. One example of LPA in the workplace is neither laughing nor even smiling at off-color jokes until the jokester understands his humor is unappreciated.

Do You Need Clarity? Write It Down.

If you're too close to a situation, or too emotional about circumstances, if you have thoughts, ideas or observations that seem contradictory or muddled in your mind, write them down. Keep a notebook handy, and put your thoughts on paper immediately.

Writing down our reactions to day-to-day issues and events around us offers many advantages. First, it takes us from our emotional right brain to our analytical left brain, giving us a clearer picture with which to make lucid decisions. The very act of structuring words, phrases and paragraphs disciplines us to be more structured in our thought process. The act of writing this book, for example, has enabled me to clarify and organize many of the concepts that for years have ambiguously floated around in my mind.

PERSUASIVE TACTICS

We live with the blessings and the curse of the Information Age. Our world is awash with information, much of it extraneous. In order for us to function effectively, our minds create short cuts to process the flood of input our minds receive each day. In today's computer-conscious times, we could call this "default thinking."

It's dinnertime. The phone rings. I answer and a voice says, "Good evening, is this Dr. John Byrnes (usually mispronounced)? How are you this evening?" Instant default thinking cuts to a conclusion: This is a sales pitch. I save both our time by responding, "Thanks, but I'm not interested," and hang up.

These short cuts can trigger either a positive or a negative response to a communication—negative in the case of the phone solicitor— especially a spoken message by one person meant to influence the thinking of another, or to persuade him to reconsider his opinion on an issue.

We as Aggression Managers must be able to use such a tactic to take an effective offense, or, defensively, recognize and respond to it appropriately in the heat of an incident of aggression. The following are Persuasion Tactics I've developed over the years. The explanations of these mental short cuts enable us to quickly process and employ, to our advantage, the following Persuasion Tactics:

Persuasive Tactic of Invoking Spite

- People are often motivated to act out of spite.
- People resent being thought of as inferior, in any way.

- Tactical Statements that invoke spite: (1)"This may be a little pricey for you, but we have some less expensive ones over there;" (2) "You may not understand what I am about to tell you."

Persuasive Tactic of Reduced Concession

- People tend to concede to a smaller demand, if they have just turned down a much greater demand.
- Tactical Statement: "If you aren't able to help me on this larger issue, certainly you can help me on this other, smaller issue."

Persuasive Tactic of False Credibility

- There are three kinds of lies: lies, huge lies and statistics.
- Humans tend to like products, services or suggestions that are endorsed by others they like or respect, whether the "others" are credible or not.
- Most people tend to agree to proposals, products, services or suggestions that will be perceived as acceptable by the majority of other people or a majority of their community.

Persuasive Tactic of the Limited Offer

- When an individual perceives that something he might want is limited in quantity, he often believes that its value is greater than if it were available in abundance.
- The harder something is to acquire, the greater the value we place on its attainment.
- No urgency, no scarcity, often produces no desire.
- Make what you are offering rare and hard to find, and you instantly increase its value.
- Tactical Statement: *"Bruto, you have worked hard to gain this important position, you may never have an opportunity like this again, why take the risk of losing it?"*

Persuasive Tactic of Reciprocity

- When someone gives you something of perceived value, you immediately respond with the desire to give something back—often something of greater value.
- People dislike the feeling of "owing."
- Beware of free offerings, they can involve either a trick or a hidden obligation.
- Tactical Statement: "I really don't have time for you today, but I am going to make an exception for you because I believe your issue is important." What do I want in return? His cooperation.

Persuasive Tactic of Creating Expectation

- Our expectations of others and ourselves play a powerful role in how we digest information and how we perform.
- When someone, whom you believe in or respect, expects you to perform a task or act in a certain way, you will tend to fulfill his expectation whether positive or negative.
- "Positive Expectations" is one of the four key ingredients of hardiness as it relates to psychoneuroimmunology. (N. Cousins, *Head First: The Biology of Hope.*)
- Tactical Statements: (1)"Stick with me, I'll make us both winners;" (2) "I know I can count on you. I know that you can do it!"

Persuasive Tactic of Contrast

- When two items are relatively different from each other, we will see them as more different if placed in close proximity of each other—either in time or space.
- If you want something to contrast starkly, show or share them together. Bring up both issues together. *"Bruto, you can enjoy watching your daughter grow up every day—or you can face the possibility of years in jail away from her. It's your choice."*
- If you want to diminish the differences between two issues place them further apart. Show one today and the other a week from

today. *"Bruto, I haven't mentioned it before, but I think you'd pre-fer being a free man, with no criminal record, and be able to watch your daughter grow up every day. I know I would."*

Persuasive Tactic of Projected Thinking

- Our mind perceives what it is conditioned to perceive.
- People see and hear exactly what they expect to see and hear, even if it differs from their actual perception. They project their views on reality so that reality changes to become what they project.
- Tactical Statements: (1)"It's perfectly clear. This ballot is valid because we can see from the dimpled chad who the voter intended to vote for;" (2) "It's perfectly clear. This ballot is invalid, because the voter did not punch a hole through the indicated area in accordance with clearly visible instructions."

Persuasive Tactic of Continuity

- Aggressors tend to react in a way that is consistent with what they perceive as truth and is a continuation of their current perspective. If you begin your persuasion from what the aggressor perceives as truth, he will more readily accept and respond to your persuasion. An example of this is a story educator John Holt tells of visiting an elementary school and observing a geography lesson. The fifth grade teacher was pointing to a wall map of the United States and was asking the students questions dealing with points of the compass. Holt, on a hunch, asked if the might ask a question. He approached the wall map, removed it, and laid it flat on the floor. He then asked the students, "Which way is north?" All the students pointed toward the ceiling! According to Antonio Damasio (1994) humans form "dispositional representations" (such as traits, values, opinions and schemas) over time, these representations are linked to "somatic markers" that register pain or pleasure when the representations are activated. (Adapted from Pierce J. Howard, Ph.D., *The Owner's Manual for the Brain, Everyday Applications from Mind-Brain Research*.) At the outset, identify what your aggressor's predispositions are and build your persuasion from them.

- If you illustrate a pattern of behavior, it is assumed that you will continue that behavior.
- Predictability gives people a sense of control and comfort, they expect and desire it. Behavior that seems to have no continuity or purpose will keep humans off-balance and cause increasing consternation.
- Tactical Statement: "You remember when I helped Jack work through a similar issue. I can do the same for you, if you will let me."

Persuasive Tactic of Acceptance by Association

- We agree with those we respect, listen to those we like.
- People tend to accept opinions or ideas endorsed by others they trust or admire.
- Tactical Statement: *"You don't have to take my word, Bruto. Ask your friends at work, those you trust, how I've always supported them—just like I want to help you now."*

Persuasive Tactic of Infectious Emotions

- Emotions are infectious: anger, panic, fear, calm

Persuasive Tactic of Reducing Isolation

- Humans are social creatures by nature. They crave contact with others.
- In moments of uncertainty and danger, you need to resist the desire to isolate yourself and seek out friends, old and new, to come to your aid.
- Isolationism can soon become a prison.
- If you see someone beginning to isolate themselves, encourage them to rely on a network of friends.

Persuasive Tactic of Fears

- By focusing on those things which cause us anguish and anxiety we give that anguish and anxiety power. We must be aware of those things that cause us anxiety but we must focus on those things that produce solutions, e.g., SolutionPerson.
- We tell bank tellers and other potential victims of armed robbery, never focus on the weapon, because you put the weapon in charge.
- When we dwell on a petty problem, we give it existence and credibility.
- People are all motivated toward pleasure and away from pain and they are more motivated by the fear of pain than the desire to seek pleasure.

Persuasive Tactic of Friends

- It is important to be perceived as a friend if you are to be successful in the persuasion process, because, when someone you like and trust asks you to do something, you want to do it.

Persuasive Tactic of Expanding on Perspective

- When an individual announces in writing or verbally that he is taking a position on any issue or point of view, he will strongly tend to defend that belief regardless of its accuracy even in the face of overwhelming evidence to the contrary.
- "Once you are a hammer, everything looks like a nail." (Abraham Maslow)
- An Aggression Manager may find it easier to convince an aggressor that he is not an aggressor, than it is to convince him not to act aggressively.

Persuasive Tactic of Peer Conformity

- People tend to agree to ideas or proposals they perceive as acceptable to the majority of others in their peer group.

- Tactical Statement: *"Bruto, I'm sure you're proud that your work team has a record of zero claims over the last five years. And everyone is working so hard to continue this excellent record."*

Persuasive Tactic of Power

- People exercise power over other people to the degree that those exercising power are perceived as having greater authority, strength or expertise.
- Unfortunately, there are still many people who are perceived as having power or strength because they threaten the use of aggression in order to get what they want.

Persuasive Tactic of Words with Power

- Use of the individual's name and preferably the first name.
- "Please" and "Thank You" tend to motivate people.
- "Don't"—people often cannot make a picture of the word "don't" in their minds, because it is not a noun. What is stated like a negative may be heard in the brain as a positive. Tactical Statements: (1) "Don't feel as though you have to buy something today;" (2)"Don't decide now, you can do it later if you're uncomfortable." May be heard as, "Decide now."
- "Might" and "Maybe" helps persuade others in a far more gentle and effective way. Tactical Statement: "You might want to consider another solution . . ."

Persuasive Tactic of Because

- Offering a reason is an effective persuasive tool. People need to hear a reason for your request. They respond much more favorably.
- Tactical Statement: "I need to go to the front of the line, because . . ." Note: Often, it is not really important what the "because" is.

Persuasive Tactic of Being Credible

- Credibility is in the eye of the perceiver.
- The first rule of credibility is never to tell another person more than he can believe.
- Be precise; i.e., the value of the painting is $1,495.85.
- The more objective you appear, the more credibility you gain.

Persuasive Tactic of Sharing Secrets

- People love secrets. When you share a secret with others, you gain a great deal of trust from your listeners.
- Tactical Statements: (1) "I shouldn't be telling you this, but . . ." (2) "Most people don't know this, but . . ."

Persuasive Tactic of Assumption of the Obvious

- When we give people credit for knowing something they know nothing about, they generally will say nothing and allow us to believe them to be smarter or more aware than they really are. Even better, your assumption of their knowledge flatters them.
- Tactical Statements: (1) "You probably already know that . . ." (2) "I don't have to tell you that . . ."

Persuasive Tactic of Framing

- People don't like to be told what to do. We like to think that each great idea is ours, and when we have some great revelation or insight, it is entirely our own.
- Tactical Statement: "I could tell you that you are making a mistake but I won't. You want to figure it out for yourself."

Persuasive Tactic of Perception as Truth

- How do we come to accept something as truth? Truth is what each individual perceives it to be. Start with the aggressor's truth and move him to your truth.

- One way someone knows you're telling the truth is that you believe the same thing he does, or come to the same conclusion. If you agree with him, then you're also right and are speaking the truth.
- Any negative statement you make about yourself is instantly accepted as a truth, whereas, a positive statement by you about yourself may be perceived dubiously.
- The key to this pattern is to get someone to either say or think, "Yes . . . yes . . . yes."
- Tactical Statements: (1)"Sometimes we move too fast to stop and say thanks, don't you think?" (2) "It's not like it used to be. So much has changed, wouldn't you agree?"

CHAPTER 6

The Art of Persuasion—Part 3

Pacing the Aggressor—Verbal Persuasion

THREE VERBAL STRATEGIES OF PERSUASION

Now you're working to strengthen a sense of trust between you and the aggressor, and to refine in your own mind the crux of the matter—or "where he's coming from." You should also be thinking of how you're going to persuade this person who appears angry, bitter, frustrated and even desperate, to come over to your side. Everything you do or say, for the duration of your discussions with the aggressor, falls into three areas of strategy: Suggestion, Impressment, and Controlling Options.

Suggestion

The strategy of Suggestion plants an idea in the mind of the aggressor. It activates his imagination of future events, or memories of past feelings or events. When you ask him, "Have you considered what would happen to you if you were to split the supervisor's head," he begins to imagine consequences. You help him along. "Think about going to jail. Think about what would happen to your family." If, on the other hand, he is losing his quality of judgment you may need to use Higher Priority Values or Suggestions, which we'll discuss later in the chapter. Using suggestion to recall past, more positive feelings, you might ask, "Remember when you first came here, how everybody worked and got along together?" This type of suggestion, called "smoothing," calls on the Aggressor to focus on the positive aspects of an issue, and can have a calming effect on the individual as he searches his memory.

Impressment

This strategy convinces the aggressor to come with you along a course of action because it is in his best interests—and *if possible,* have him believe that it is his idea. Both Suggestion and Controlling Options are strategies that lead to Impressment, which involves a final decision to take the action you want the aggressor to take. Effective Impressment preserves dignity and sense of pride. Humiliation of the aggressor should *never* be the aim of any persuasion.

Controlling Options

This strategy enables the aggressor to select an option for action, as long as it is the option you want him to select. You must decide whether the aggressor responds more readily to a logical or emotionally based approach. One aggressor might select an option because otherwise he will automatically lose his job; another, because he will disappoint and embarrass his family. The Aggression Manager provides the aggressor with options that allow him to believe he is making his own decision, without losing his dignity, e.g., "Here's why you should do what I've suggested. If you decide to become aggressive, company policy, in the interest of safety, will force us to terminate you. So the choice is really up to you, isn't it?" "Setting limits" is a technique of controlling options. The limits you set must be clearly stated. "Bruto, if you hit him, you *will* be arrested for assault. But if you walk away now, maybe we can forget this whole thing." When laying out the options, always save *your* option for last, because the final option stated always makes the most impact. Limits must be enforceable as well. "If you do this, company policy states you must be terminated. It's not my choice; it's yours to make." And limits must be reasonable. Don't make any promises you can't keep. "If you stop now, I'll talk to the division manager about your situation. But it's your decision."

DETERMINING THE CRUX OF THE MATTER

At the outset, as you work to gain the trust of an aggressor, you need to be sizing up the individual. So ask yourself several questions:

- Where is he coming from? What is his agenda?
- What has he got to gain if he continues on this aggressive path? (This appeals to the aggressor motivated "toward something.")
- What has he got to lose? (This appeals to the aggressor motivated "away from something.")
- How can I use the answers to the first three questions to dissuade him from continuing his aggressive course?

FIVE TYPES OF QUESTIONS

The answers to the Crux of the Matter can be determined by asking the aggressor questions? You can only ask five types of questions, some good, some not so good:

- Open Questions (sometimes referred to as open-ended questions)—Good choice. Since you want the aggressor to open up and give you information from his perspective, an open question is any that requires him to explain or expound on an issue that is on his mind. These are typically "What," "Why" and "When" questions that draw him out from behind his wall of anger or frustration. "What" or "Why" question might be inflammatory when referring to the aggressor or his actions. If possible, use a "When" question that deflects blame and may sound less judgmental. "Jane, when did you begin feeling anxious about this issue?" "Bruto, are you so unhappy here that you'd threaten someone?"
- Closed Questions (sometimes referred to as closed-ended questions)—Bad choice. These are any questions that the aggressor can answer with a simple "Yes" or "No." They allow him to stay behind the wall, and are counterproductive to your objective of getting to the Crux of the Matter. "This isn't the way to solve your problem, is it?"
- Probing Questions—Good choice. These questions are often follow-ups to your initial open questions, in that they delve deeper into an issue after it has been exposed by the aggressor. Probing questions are also open questions. "Bruto, how do you think you could have handled your frustration without hurting Louise's feelings?"

- Leading Questions—Good choice only after you have determined the Crux of the Matter. After you believe you've reached the Crux of the Matter, confirm your conclusion in the form of a leading question. "So, Bruto, if I understand what you've been saying, the real issue here is your resentment that after 16 years of service in the company, promotions are going to younger people. Isn't that correct?" It is a bad choice to use a leading question to identify the crux of the matter.
- Loaded Questions—Never a good choice. Never ask loaded questions, because they incriminate or belittle the aggressor, force him to admit he is at fault or even insult him. "Bruto, isn't this the dumbest thing you've ever done?" Again, such a question would undermine your pursuit of the Crux of the Matter and probably end your ability to persuade this aggressor away from his aggression.

Just as important as the type of question you ask is what you do *after* asking the question. You shut up! Remember that your task is to draw information out of the aggressor, not keep him quiet by doing all the talking yourself. The individual has used aggressive actions to make a statement he perhaps could not make verbally, or that no one seemed interested in hearing. You demonstrate your interest by listening.

That brings us to the power of silence. Negotiating experts who train executives teach them that silence can be golden indeed. A skilled contract negotiator can make thousands of dollars of difference in contract terms by saying . . . nothing.

We Americans are uncomfortable with silence. We're gregarious and talkative by nature, perhaps because we have a national need to be liked. When American business people began negotiating with the Japanese and later the Chinese, they discovered how uncomfortable silence could be. The executives across the table in Tokyo or Beijing were perfectly content to sit quietly for an extended period of time, as they maintain eye contact with their opponents, letting silence do their work for them. The typical American reaction is to fill that silence, all too often with inappropriate concessions just to get the other parties talking again.

During an aggressive situation, the aggressor may want to talk. So when you ask him a question, be silent and let him fully complete his answer. And after he has finished his initial answer, you may feel he has more to say, so remain quiet. Let silence work. He may have the urge to fill it with more information you need to bring the incident to a successful close.

Your skillful use of open and probing questions and silence should give you some answers about what is really going on in the aggressor's mind, what is important to him and what he values. Once you have this information, you have key leverage to use in further discussion.

USING SUGGESTION TO TAKE THE INITIATIVE

Earlier we listed Suggestion as one of the three strategies of persuasion, the strategy that plants an idea you want planted in the aggressor's mind. We mentioned *smoothing* as a technique during our discussion of Suggestion, in that we suggest focusing on the positive aspects of an issue. There are three other techniques you can use to deploy Suggestion, and to take the initiative in bringing about a mental change in the aggressor's mind:

- Reframing—Dignity is the last rational thing to go. Once dignity is cast aside, the aggressor has no place to go but over the precipice of self-destruction and violence. Reframing is a technique that helps to restore dignity after the aggressor has taken an undignified action. It suggests a more positive or more honorable motive for an individual to have acted aggressively. "Bruto, maybe the real reason you've acted this way is that your own standards of quality were frustrated by the rush we've been working under."
- Triangling—An aggressor usually focuses his anger on an individual, because the individual is the tangible representation of a policy, an organization or a situation the aggressor can't get his hands on, or perhaps can't even grasp mentally. He can't attack an intangible, so he "transfers" or goes after a person or a group of persons, or in the case of sabotage, equipment, computer systems or an entire building. More to the point, he might focus that anger on you. Triangling deflects his anger back toward the abstract idea. "Bruto, I don't understand a lot about the new policy either, I am

here to help you work through it. . . ." "Bruto, some of the guidelines probably seem unfair to old-timers like us, I want to help you
see this from their perspective. . . ." A triangle has three sides,
you, the aggressor and an abstract villain. Your challenge is to
transfer his anger from you, others or your organization toward an
abstract villain, like policy or guidelines, etc., who he cannot physically attack.

- Cooling off—This is "taking a break" to let a heated situation
  cool. If possible, invite the aggressor out of the room or area in
  which he has created the aggressive incident. "Let's go get a cup
  of coffee," or "Let's go for a walk, I need to stretch my legs."
  Cooling off is a technique to leave the problem in one room while
  you and the aggressor go into another. Once the two of you make
  a "change of scenery," you have an opportunity to build rapport
  and trust. So change the subject away from the conflictive issue
  toward personal interests. "Got any kids?" "Got any pictures of
  them?" "Did you see the game last night?" Having developed an
  added measure of rapport and trust, you can now return to the
  room where the problem has remained, and address it with a much
  better chance of solving it.

You can also take a break to separate yourself, leaving the aggressor
alone in the room. This is a prudent move if you perceive yourself
becoming part of the problem. Say, "Bruto, would you excuse me for
a couple of minutes. I have to visit the restroom." This gives the
aggressor some moments to cool down, and gives you a chance to ask
for help from associates, coordinate signals for a possible team intervention or notify the police if you feel the situation warrants such
action.

There may be an incident in which two employees may be yelling at
one another and threatening each other with bodily harm. Typically,
people do not want to fight. Fighting is a repugnant notion to most
adults who relate it to pain, blood and torn clothes. But two employees
standing nose to nose trading insults may force themselves to fight
unless an *objective* third party, whom they both respect, separates
them.

When the appropriate party (you for example) separates them, neither person loses face by having backed down. In fact, though they will never admit it, they're grateful for your action. But remember—even though you might agree or disagree with either party, you *must* remain neutral, and be seen as acting in both their best interests.

PARAPHRASING AND "PARROT-PHRASING"

People like nothing better than to hear someone else repeat what they themselves have said. It is as if the playback of a statement by another lends it credibility, memorializes it, gives it more import—and by implication boosts the importance of its author.

This is just as true with the aggressor who makes a threat or any statement in the heat of anger or frustration, or as a tactic to back the Aggression Manager down a notch. Being a trained Aggression Manager, however, you have a defensive tactic of your own. You can use the repetition of the statement, however irresponsible or off-the-wall, as an effective defensive countermeasure—with paraphrasing *or* with "parrot-phrasing."

With both techniques, you have the aggressor's attention because he is listening to his own words. And as long as he is listening, you have control. Just as important, when you thoughtfully repeat his words, whether they're a threat or a statement of his demands, you create empathy.

When you "parrot-phrase," repeating his words using the same tone, you come across as a person who cares and respects enough about what the aggressor has stated to repeat it, to make sure you understood it. "Let me see if I understand what you've said, Bruto. You want us to let you keep your job, transfer you to shipping and give you Thursday afternoons off. Is that what you said?"

Paraphrasing has an additional objective. In addition to repeating the aggressor's words, it uses tone of voice and body language to change intent. Experts in behavioral science tell us that words themselves only convey 7% of a spoken message. Tone of voice carries 38% of a communication, and body language 55%. That means every utterance from "What are you doing here?" to "I can't wait to see Aunt Sally" can mean many things depending on tone of voice and body language. It is important to note that, when body language and words clash, the aggressor will typically rely on your body language for their interpretation. If establishing credibility, making an initial impression and building a bridge of trust with the aggressor are important, your body language will have the greatest impact.

In our context, an aggressor shouts, "I've already told Johnson I'm going to break his leg the next time I see him!"

You *don't* say, "That's a stupid thing you've said. You're not going to do that." He might jump up and go break Johnson's leg just to prove a point. So you paraphrase. But instead of parroting his exact words, you lean forward with obvious concern, and speak slowly with mild shock and disbelief.

"Did I hear right? You're going to actually break Johnson's leg?"

Your tone of voice and body language are saying to the aggressor, "Your statement is ridiculous and unacceptable," while your actual question opens an opportunity for the aggressor to reconsider what he has just said, soften it and to back away from his threat without losing his dignity.

"Aw, well, I probably wouldn't break his leg, but he is such a jerk."

Your reaction also implies that what the aggressor is considering is unfair to Johnson, no matter what perceived injustice Johnson has done to the aggressor.

Fairness is a peculiarly important American trait. All our lives we heard "What's fair is fair" and "We've got to be fair." People pride themselves on their sense of fairness or "fair play." So when you deal with an aggressor, usually you're talking to an aggrieved individual who, for all his anger, has maintained an innate sense of fairness.

Paraphrasing opens the door for a compromise in the interest of fairness. "Look, instead of you breaking Johnson's leg, why don't I suggest that his supervisor talk to him about you. Johnson will know how you feel about things—and you won't be arrested for assault. Isn't that fair?"

Another value of paraphrasing, in the event of bystanders, is to enable them to focus on the aggressor's statements—especially if they're threats. At this point you need to play to those bystanders, so that their facial expressions mirror the surprise and concern in your tone of voice. ("Man, did you hear what he just said?") Why? Because when you see the looks on their faces at hearing his threatening statement, you know that the bystanders have become your witnesses.

INSULTS

As he does with emotional weighting, the angry aggressor will try to make you as angry as he is by insulting you, your capabilities, looks, lineage, manhood or womanhood. He may also use the foulest, most vile language he can articulate. He wants to unnerve and rattle you, and bring you down to his level in the arena. An aggressor who is unable to articulate his issues will try to move you away from your reason, rational thinking and logic by insulting you personally in order to spike your emotions. If he succeeds in spiking your emotions with his insults, he wins. Emotions are potent, fast-acting triggers, which distract us from our logic, reason and rationale.

An old Asian text says, "When an aggressor throws a spear of insult at your head, move your head. The spear misses the target, and leaves the aggressor empty-handed. And the spear is in the wall, not you." Translated, that means bite your tongue and toughen your hide. Your best defensive strategy against insults is deflection. You can use "strip phrasing" to strip his insult of its power by moving quickly beyond it.

"I hear what you're saying. However, the larger picture is . . ."

"I understand that, Bruto, but . . ."

"Yeah, I probably am a jerk, however right now we need to focus on . . ."

Deflection of an insult keeps it impersonal to you. It also becomes a springboard back to the real issue. "But right now we have to work out something more important. . . ." Just as crucial, deflection takes the emotional steam out of the aggressor's insult. His insults and other verbal abuse are meant to inflame your emotions and sidetrack your efforts. Since those insults aren't effecting your determination to end an aggressive situation, you are disempowering him with every deflection. Also, remember the strategies suggested in emotional weighting once you have deflected this aggressor.

BACK TO THE AGGRESSION CONTINUUM—AND MOUNTING ANXIETY

In earlier chapters, we discussed at some length the Aggression Continuum, that handy thermometer with which we can evaluate how far along the aggressor is before he may become violent. The Continuum is also, by the way, an excellent template you can use for organizing your thoughts and recalling the sequence of events if and when you must write a report of the incident or testify in court.

Referring back to our Continuum, you can see that the Escalation Phase, during which you are using your Aggression Management skills, manifests itself in the aggressor as a time of "mounting anxiety." The aggressor expresses his anxiety with verbal aggression, employing four offensive tactics, for which you must have defenses.

Verbal Aggression during Mounting Anxiety

- Questioning Your Authority—The aggressor questions an instruction, request or directive you have given. He may growl, "Who are you to tell me to do anything?" He must understand that he can question a task, but not your authority. As with insults, use strip phrasing to step out of the way almost as if you didn't hear him, and remove the energy from his question. "I understand your feelings, however the bigger issue here is . . . ."

- Refusal—The aggressor refuses to do or say what you've asked him to do. "Forget it, man!" Your immediate response is to employ the technique of setting limits, or offering *clear, reasonable* and *enforceable* choices that provide apparent options.

   "Bruto, you can put down the hammer with no consequences, or you can continue to threaten us. But I must tell you that if you don't put it down, in the interest of safety, company policy states you must be terminated. The choice is really yours to make. It's your decision. It's up to you."

- Verbal Release—At some point, perhaps midway along the Aggression Continuum, the aggressor will no longer be able to contain the pressure of mounting anxiety. A small confrontation, a harsh word, maybe just a hostile glance will set him off. In an instant, the aggressor's veneer of civility disappears in a torrent of verbal abuse that gives vent to pent up rage.

Typically, an aggressor will begin to regain his quality of judgment once he has vented. So I recommend that you let him vent. During this unpleasant time, don't try to stop him, or "shush" him from disturbing others. Let him yell. Instead, you might want to cycle breathe, (I will teach you cycle breathing in chapter 8) so that your adrenaline level doesn't rise to match his and your mind remains clear and focused. Usually, the aggressor shouts only until he runs out of breath. But during this display of anger, you need to remember that your safety and that of others is at risk.

Let him say what he wants now, as long as he does what you say. When he is thoroughly vented, emotionally drained and begins to regain his quality of judgment, approach him quietly and remove him gently to another area, so the two of you can "move forward together" to solve his problems. Later, after the individual has fully regained his self-control and judgment, as a supervisor you may have to deal with the content of what he has said.

- Intimidation—This is the most advanced, most serious escalation of verbal aggression in the Mounting Anxiety Phase of the Continuum. With intimidation and threats, the aggressor is at the threshold of the Crisis Phase.

First and foremost, *take all threats seriously*. Here is an example of why I say that. In 1992, a man named Clifton McKee was terminated from his job in Ft. Lauderdale, Florida. For 14 months, he emotionally stewed over the fact that he had been fired. During those months, he made repeated threats, telling a number of people he was going to kill those responsible for his being fired. After 14 months, he walked into his former place of employment and shot five supervisors dead. Afterward, everyone said something like, "Well, he did mention several times that he was going to kill them, but I didn't think he'd really do it."

Not only do you take an aggressor's threat seriously, but also you let him know immediately and unequivocally that you must take action if he indeed means his threat. So you use paraphrasing to clarify the intensity of his threat, leaning toward him to emphasize your seriousness.

"Bruto please let me understand this. If you're stating that you intend to blow Johnson's brains out, this would be a serious threat. Our company now has a zero tolerance policy on threats, so if you mean it I would have to take immediate action. So I can get it correct in my mind, would you please restate what you said, only more slowly?"

The aggressor may realize that he has overplayed his use of intimidation, and back down. How you deal with him at that point depends on how sincere you think his recant is. If however he repeats the threat, notify security and/or call the police. Then as soon as you can, regardless of whether or not he reconsiders his threat, document your conversation with the aggressor in writing and provide a copy to the appropriate supervisor.

THINGS YOU NEVER SAY TO AN AGGRESSOR

One element of building trust is to avoid intentionally or unintentionally demeaning or belittling the aggressor. Here are some statements that would confirm in his mind that no one understands or cares about his problem. Remember—behavior scientists tell us the 7% of all communication is in words, and 38% is in tone of voice. That means that *how you say your words* is five times more important than the words themselves. To make matters worse, these statements are usually made in a condescending tone of voice.

- "Come here!"
- "You wouldn't understand." (The tone implies "stupid")
- "Because those are the rules."
- "It's none of your business."
- "What do you want me to do about it?"
- "Would you calm down!"
- "What's your problem?"
- "You never . . ." or "You always . . ."
- "I'm not going to say this again."
- "I'm doing this for your own good."
- "Why don't you be reasonable?"

THINGS YOU CAN SAY TO AN AGGRESSOR

For you to be an effective Aggression Manager you must verbally de-escalate an aggressor. To do so there are three key ingredients:

- Respect—we must demonstrate respect to the aggressor. "But wait," you say, "I don't even like this person. Are you telling me I have to show him respect?" That's right. Your safety and the safety of those in your care are at risk. If you wish to be an effective persuader, you must demonstrate respect.
- Acknowledgment of the aggressor's feelings. (This is self-explanatory.)
- Offer the aggressor some brief sense of validation: How do you achieve these three ingredients? "You seem upset. Please repeat what you just said, only more slowly!" When you ask him to repeat himself, you're implying that you respect the aggressor enough to get it right the first time. When you say, "You seem upset." You are offering a brief sense of validation and acknowledging his feelings.

Verbal Strategy

- Phrases that are de-escalating: "Let me understand . . . ," "Allow me to help . . . ," "Please tell me more . . ." or "Because . . ." Any phrase beginning with *Let*, *Allow* or *Please* are positive. They declare your intent to be part of the solutions. As we discussed in the Persuasive Tactic of Because in chapter 5, the word *because* is also a very powerful word. Humans need to hear a "Because . . ." and will respond favorably to it. What is particularly interesting is, they will respond favorably to almost any "because." So, offer a "Because . . ."
- Use words with strong positive connotations: One destructive illustration was when the Heaven's Gate cult convinced all of those people to commit suicide by referring to their bodies as "containers." Euphemisms are often used to take the sting out of emotionally charged words like the phrase "peacekeeper" for a military campaigns and when civilian casualties are termed "collateral

damage." Words with strong connotations can be plucked right out of their intended use and placed in any number of other uses with almost as much strength of connotation. *Racism* is one of those words. It is a very emotionally and politically charged word. An individual can use that word in almost any context and it will emotionally move its audience, whether the term is justified or not. Some positively connotative words are: compassion, fairness, caring, respectful, righteous, challenge, choice, dream, family, pride, reform, unique, passionate, and strength. Some positive connotative words which are known to motivate: benefit, guarantee, money, results, easy, health, safe, free, how to, save, love, proven, and you or your.

- Use words that deflect aggression: Certain words incite aggression like "Why" or "What:" "Why, did you do that?! "What is wrong with you?"; *whereas a word like* "When" *can deflects aggression* "When did you start feeling this way?"
- Don't tell them what you can't do or what you will try to do. It is more compelling to tell them what you can do. "Here is what I can do . . ."
- If someone is using sniping behavior it is important to note that partial truth is far more dangerous than a total lie. Sometimes an excellent response is to either make a statement that is outrageous, "Yes, I did turn away from him, not in anger, but in fear, because I was afraid of turning into a pillar of salt," so that the partial truth will be discounted, or you should expose the complete truth.
- If an aggressor uses verbally abusive behavior, don't take possession of his problem. The use of words like "me," "my," "I" and "mine" indicate that you are taking this statement personally, for example, "*I'm* hurt by what you have said," "You've insulted *me* by your comments." Phrases like "This seems to have upset you . . ." or "I understand that you are upset . . ." can help.
- If an aggressor exhibits physically threatening behavior, sometimes the use of self-deprecating explanations will help: "You're right, I'm sorry, I couldn't be more wrong."

Some other excellent phrases are:

- "You might want to back up. If I breathe on you, you'll be sick for a month." *This is one of my favorite statements, if someone is in your face.*
- "Thank you for sharing your concerns with me."
- "I don't know the answer to that, but I will get the information for you." Sometimes the aggressor just needs to know that someone is working on his behalf.
- "We made a mistake; I apologize. What can we do to put it right?" You may not be at fault, but this emerging aggressor needs to hear an apology.
- "I'm not here to add to your concerns, I want to be part of the solution." This is an excellent statement of purpose. It establishes the "SolutionPerson" based framework for your discussions. Aggressors find it difficult to get aggressive with someone who is genuinely trying to help.

CHAPTER 7

The Art of Persuasion—Part 4

Pacing the Aggressor—Non-Verbal Persuasion

NON-VERBAL (MANUAL) PACING

Up until now we've been discussing Pacing the Aggressor through verbal persuasion. But as you may recall, 55% of communication is transmitted through body language. Accordingly, you can pull alongside the aggressor to take quiet control with some skillful use of non-verbal or manual pacing techniques.

Non-verbal communication, of course, is two-way communication. Both of you send continuous non-verbal signals to one another, consciously and unconsciously. Your task is to recognize and read his signals. They are valuable feedback to help you determine where he is on the Aggression Continuum, and whether or not he is telling you the truth. Simultaneously, you send your own non-verbal signals to reassure the aggressor of your non-threatening role, and to slide gradually toward controlling his actions and thought processes.

Feedback—A Human Need

As social animals we humans need feedback from other humans. We crave the satisfaction of knowing that our communications are being received by another mind. One extreme example is that the United States government is spending millions of dollars transmitting signals into deep space, hoping to receive a reply from intelligent life on some distant planet. At the opposite extreme, the worst punishment a prisoner can receive is isolation in solitary confinement. As we've learned from returning prisoners of war, an individual locked away for weeks or years in isolation must fabricate a world of feedback or slide into madness.

Types of Non-Verbal Feedback

In your dealings with an aggressor, you know you're going to get verbal and non-verbal feedback. While verbal feedback gives you facts, figures and words that express feelings and information, non-verbal feedback conveys genuine emotions, moods and feelings that words might try to conceal.

Non-verbal feedback can tell us where the aggressor is on the Aggression Continuum, so we can respond appropriately. We've already discussed the four areas of verbal aggression—Questioning, Refusal, Verbal Release and Intimidation, and how we elicit verbal information through questioning. Now let's discuss the types and value of non-verbal feedback.

There are several types of non-verbal feedback that fall into three main categories—*deliberate, instinctive* and *physiological.*

Deliberate

Deliberate Gesticulation   This includes all conscious gestures and mannerisms, primarily using hands and arms, that reinforce a verbal message, such as shaking a fist, pounding a fist in the palm of the other hand or pointing a finger at the listener. These are threatening gestures often used by the aggressor, but never to be used by you as an Aggression Manager. You also want to avoid deliberate palms down or facing out gestures. These can indicate dominance and commands, e.g., "Just calm down. Hold it!" Instead, you use your hands with palms up, a nonthreatening, submissive signal that says in effect, "Please . . . help me help you."

Deliberate Expression   Conscious facial expressions. A smile to indicate approval or satisfaction—or to mask anger. A genuine, sincere smile can be the best non-verbal expression used with an aggressor. It expresses a quiet confidence, an enthusiasm to solve an issue, a happiness to be there to help in the solution, and the appearance of an almost unconditional acceptance of the aggressor and his issues.

Good poker players are masters at using facial expression, or lack of expression, to send false signals to other players. (Have you ever smiled slightly when you were dealt a bad hand so you wouldn't wince?) We humans express more emotions facially than any other animal, and enjoy doing so.

(As an aside, pity the poor crocodile. I tell my seminars the crocodile has but four expressions in his entire inventory—open mouth/open eyes, open mouth/closed eyes, closed mouth/open eyes and closed mouth/closed eyes.)

As we become more global in our outlook, we need to be aware that all deliberate expressions are not universal in meaning. We Americans automatically flash the "A-Okay!" with our thumb and forefinger. "How's your steak, sir?" "A-Okay!"

In Southern France, that hand gesture can mean "Zero" or "No good," so your waiter will be insulted by your intended "A-Okay." In Japan, that gesture makes reference to money, so you may be telling your waiter your steak is too expensive. And in parts of Latin America and the Middle East, your seemingly harmless "A-Okay" translates to a body part and might put you in personal peril.

Cultural differences constitute a whole separate book. If your organization has a growing multicultural face, you may want to learn more about some of the subtleties of various cultures, in the event your next aggressor comes from a different ethnic or cultural background from your own.

Instinctive

Instinctive Gesticulation   These unconscious gestures are residue from our primal past. The aggressor may cross his arms or legs, bundling up in a defensive position as if to protect vital organs from attack. He may use his hand to cover his mouth or stroke his chin to disguise a lie. He may squirm in discomfort at his own attempts to deceive or tap his feet in agitation. A more symmetrical body language can be perceived as tense, anxious and potentially threatening. Therefore when your body language is asymmetrical, you are perceived as relaxed, calm and quietly confident, all-important messages to project.

Barrier Signaling   Instinctive gestures, in fact, begin the moment you face the aggressor, even before the two of you have positioned yourselves to talk. *Barrier signaling* is a means of saying, "You're crossing into my territory." If you enter the aggressor's office, shop or work area, he may step back or stand up, step behind a chair, cross his arms or send *all* these signals. Acknowledge that you're entering his territory by seeking permission. "May I come in?" "May I have a few minutes of your time?" Or simply nod and smile in acknowledgement of his domain.

This territorial response may extend to a piece of equipment the aggressor has spent a lot of time working with or simply floor space. In one bulk mail center, I discovered that territory was so important that different color tapes on the floor delineated the various areas of supervision.

One last tip on instinctive gesticulation in a group setting. As in the wild where the dominant animal gestures least, the dominant individual in a crowd of aggressors is often the quietest and least animated. Like the lion that stands quietly amid the pride, his mere presence is enough. Remember, your objective is to remove the dominant individual from his group of admirers. And if you need another clue about who is in charge, as you begin to talk with individuals in the group, they will glance back to the leader for approval and guidance.

Instinctive Expression   You have the makings of a great poker player if you can remain totally stone-faced while you're riding an emotional roller coaster. The lips purse in anger and the jaws tighten. The eyebrows, especially, are still driven by ancient instincts. They fly up in amazement or surprise, as if to give the eyes more room to see sudden danger. They lower to protect narrowing eyes as a growing threat is perceived. The eyes themselves dart about in discomfort, as if seeking paths of escape. The pupils constrict while the eyes fixate on a person's body to make it an object, a target of imminent attack. These expressions are tied more directly to the *autonomic nervous system* (ANS) and therefore are far more difficult to manipulate, making them more reliable as indicators of aggression. Some of the types of emotions illustrated through instinctive facial expressions are: happiness, fear, anger, disgust, sadness and distress. These are the same regardless of age, sex, race or culture.

In fact, as an Aggression Manager, you can usually determine how to best communicate with an aggressor by observing their instinctive eye movements.

1) If the aggressor tends to look up while he is responding to a question, he comprehends best at the "seeing level," picturing ideas in his mind. He might respond by saying, "I see what you're saying," "What she wants is hazy to me" or "I get the picture." Communicate to him in word pictures so he assimilates your message faster.

2) If his eyes drift from side to side, they're essentially resting while he comprehends at the "hearing level," using his auditory skills to ingest the meaning of your words. He might say, "That sounds right," "I hear what you're saying" or "That rings a bell." Apply voice volume, tone and cadence to your message carefully, because he is absorbing every word you say. Words with strong connotations will have a special impact on this aggressor.

3) If he looks down as he considers your question, he is receiving your message at the "feeling level," absorbing it tactilely. He might respond with, "That feels about right," or "Give me a concrete example," "I'm trying to grasp what you mean" or "I'm still struggling with that problem." This individual is motivated by touch. Although we've learned to be careful about touching others, this person will appreciate a genuine handshake.

Physiological

Deception, Can You Identify It?   The aggressor may try to conceal or disguise his real feelings or even the truth from you by minimizing his gesticulation. Outward calm may be hiding inner panic that he may give away the real truth. Watch for *non-verbal leakage*. These are gestures or behaviors that betray the aggressor's true feelings or intent despite his best efforts to deceive you.

If he is lying, often he may cross his arms or legs as if to keep the truth from spilling out. He may also make his story longer and more convoluted if he is trying to weave a lie. If he is telling the truth, he is more likely to use free, natural gestures, while his story is shorter and more to the point. Truth takes less time to tell than fabrication. Liars often smile less; when liars smile typically it is forced, their smiles linger and end abruptly. Liars find it difficult to keep eye contact, when cues for the mouth and eyes clash, the eyes prevail. Confident, honest humans stand erect or sit up straight. Liars tend to slouch and put their hands in their pockets when sitting. They also tend to mumble and speak with less expression.

Physiological Feedback   The body itself becomes a very "talkative" source of feedback during a high-intensity personal experience. As we've discussed in earlier chapters, adrenaline kicks in and prepares the body for "fight or flight." An aggressor begins to perspire. He swallows more frequently. His breathing becomes shallow and rapid, his pupils constrict, his blink rate decreases, his face turns red with anger and veins become more prominent in the head, neck and throat. These types of feedback are tied more to our *autonomic nervous system* (ANS) and therefore are far more difficult for the aggressor to manipulate. Even if he were aware of these signs of mounting anxiety, he would probably not know how to counteract them. This makes this type of feedback more reliable as an indicator of aggression.

But you do know how to counteract them. Cycle breathing, as we'll show you in chapter 8, will keep you from matching his adrenaline-pumped physiological state with one of your own. Your mind will remain clear, your reason intact and your ability to out think the aggressor will keep you in control.

Moving the Aggressor with Non-Verbal Cues

Set up to begin talking with an aggressor in a quiet neutral office or corner. You sit down, offering him a seat, and he will sit down as well. The very act of sitting represents de-escalation. Then observe him as you continue to communicate. Is he sitting with his arms folded in front of him? Is he hunched forward or stretched back in the chair? Is he sitting with his legs crossed or are his legs open? However he is positioned, sit to his side or at a 45% angle of where he is seated, and begin to subtly mirror his actions. Cross your legs or arms just as he has done. You will be Pacing the Aggressor.

A psychologist I know tells how, during sessions with patients, he observes their posture, movements and whether they talk fast or slow. He even identifies their breathing pattern and blinking rate. He begins to emulate his patient's body language, echoing their posture and speech patterns. He will breathe like them at the same pace, and blink when they blink. When he feels that he has made a pacing connection, he leans forward. When his patient leans forward in response, he gets confirmation of that connection, and knows his ability to persuade this patient is significantly enhanced. Why? Because we all like to be connected to others, part of a larger organism. It can be an organism of 2 people in a private office, 20,000 hand clappers at a concert, or 200,000 chanting activists at an outdoors political rally.

Did you ever watch a "wave" develop in the stands at a football game? Have you ever seen anyone in a crowd of thousands resist participating in the wave? It is really a study in group dynamics, in which virtually every individual becomes a cell in the larger organism. That same dynamic works when you begin to match the movements of the aggressor.

As the two of you continue to talk, uncross your arms and put them to your side. He will unconsciously take your cue and do the same. Then uncross your legs and assume a more relaxed position. He will do the same. As he moves more and more to your cadence, he will begin to agree more and more with what you're saying, and you're on your way to resolution of the incident. The more relaxed you appear, the more relaxed he becomes. The more asymmetrical your body, the more relaxed you appear. The more relaxed the aggressor becomes, the more he will de-escalate; we are all hardwired this way.

YOU CAN SUCCEED, BUT . . .

Over the course of this chapter, we've covered a long list of strategies, tactics and techniques to help you succeed in moving an aggressor away from violence, and lowering his intensity level on the Aggression Continuum. Your knowledge and skills of Aggression Management strategies, and your courage and determination to resolve an aggressive incident will give you a high probability of success, possibly saving lives.

But no strategy will work every time. You may encounter an individual who has made the commitment to destroy others and himself, figuratively pulling the building down around him in some sort of Samson-like tragic finale. As you've heard in the news over and over, many of the most violent shooting incidents end in suicide. If you realize from your training he is about to attack you physically, you need to know how to get out his way without resorting to violence of your own.

These techniques constitute the Art of Safe Escape.

CHAPTER 8

The Art of Safe Escape

No matter how much you prepare, no matter how much you persuade, there will be times when all you can do is not enough. This chapter presupposes that every incident of aggression will not end peaceably. Some individuals have already predetermined to take their confrontation to the level of physical violence, and no amount of skillful persuasion will change their mind.

In a situation where personal danger is imminent, we must understand that adrenaline, nature's "fight or flight" enhancer, can actually be counterproductive for Aggression Managers in the face of peril. How do we control our natural rush of adrenaline in response? What's more, in today's dangerous and litigious society, "fight" is simply not an option.

Once upon a time when two people got into a fight, once the fisticuffs settled the question, both combatants dusted themselves off and headed home. Now they may go to their vehicles, retrieve their nine-millimeter handguns and return. Even if you win, in our litigious world, you can still become a civil or even criminal victim. That means that the astute Aggression Manager, besides attempting to control and direct the course of a tense situation, must also maintain control of his or her own environment. Then, if "flight" becomes the final option, he or she can affect a safe escape out of harm's way.

First, it's essential that we be aware of our environment. Whether we're at home, at work, in a local restaurant or just out on the town, we should be aware of our exits, what tools are available to us and who might we enlist to help us. This is not paranoia but simple awareness. Every time you board a commercial aircraft, you're reminded to locate the nearest exit in case of an emergency. Why not elsewhere as well?

If you went into a restaurant with your family and it caught fire, where would you and your family go to escape safely? What is an exit? A window, perhaps? How about a third story window?

How about, instead of a fire, it's a robbery. What if someone is shooting? Depending on what's below, a jump from that third story window might be preferable to becoming a target. One picture that is indelibly struck in my mind is that boy being dragged to safety out of the second story window during the shooting at Columbine High School.

MAKING PARTNERS

Who is available to help? In the military and law enforcement when an individual finds himself in a bind who does he turn to for help? His *partner*. We suggest that you make partners; people who, by use of a signal like tugging the ear, are alerted to provide or call for help. Can you make a partner on the spot? Sure you can, but isn't it much better to have worked out a plan far in advance so when the time for help arrives you have a clear picture of what you want and when you want it?

While you watch the escalating aggressor closely, you're also scanning the room to review your escape route. Because you're trained, you've positioned yourself near an open door to the hallway. Also by design, a sofa, chair or other furniture separates you from the aggressor. By a previously devised plan, two or three fellow employees are waiting to assist you just beyond the door, listening for your prearranged signal or for your rush to escape.

Let's discuss the layout of your office, workspace or classroom. Often a simple rearrangement of an office can enhance your opportunity to escape safety. In Figure 8.1 you can see, in the upper left corner, the typical office arrangement. If your objective is to escape from an exploding aggressor this is the worst possible arrangement. You have to get past the desk only to be confronted by the aggressor who stands between you and the door. An arrangement like the upper right might be far more suitable. Who gets first access to the door? You do! I especially like the idea of the occupant of this office turning to the guest and welcoming him. This not only starts the process on a positive note,

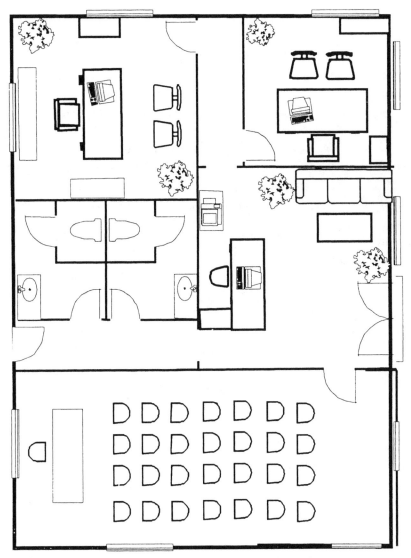

Figure 8.1 *Choosing the High Ground Illustration (Created by or for Dr. John D. Byrnes)*

but also subliminally states to the guest, "this is my territory and you will act accordingly."

As we see in the classroom layout at the bottom of the graphic, we often find teacher putting their desk at the far end of the classroom away from the entrance. I also regularly hear teachers complain that students enter into their classroom making intimidating remarks so as to take control of their class. I suggest that teachers place their desks near the entrance to the class and welcome the students into their class. Why? Subliminally you are telling them that this class/territory is yours and you expect your students to act accordingly. If you have a possible aggressor in your class you can invite him to the front, using manual pacing, as described in chapter 7. You can even move him out of the class and lock the door behind you if necessary. As you step out into the hall, you may signal to a partner (hall monitor, next class teacher, etc.) that you need assistance.

I had a nationally known organization contact me explaining that a whole department was being laid off. Thirty-one individuals were losing their jobs. Two of these individuals were known as Exploders and they wanted their exit interview with the director of Human Resources. I suggested that he greet each of these Exploders separately and in the reception area. The reception area offered lots of means of safe escape as well as a built-in partner, the receptionist, who could respond to a prearranged signal. I also suggested that he hire professional security, someone dressed just like everyone else, who would appear as though he was waiting for an appointment. How would the aggressor know that this professional security individual was paid, trained and cued to take control at a moment's notice. These precautions can be applied to virtually any workstation to reduce the possibility of aggression or provide a safe escape.

Projecting yourself into a real time incident in the Crisis Phase of the Aggression Continuum, there may be several elements that you as an Aggression Manager must assess virtually simultaneously. Put yourself face-to-face with an angry worker in a mid-sized office. After prolonged negotiation, using every verbal and non-verbal technique of persuasion at your command, you're now alone with a man who is reaching such a level of rage that he is reduced to inarticulate growling. His face is red and turning white with rage, his neck and temple veins bulging, and your training tells you he is seconds from striking at you with all his strength.

Meanwhile, you continue to talk, to try and dissuade him and play for time. You recognize by his shallow, rapid breathing, sudden silence and clenched fists that the aggressor's adrenaline is preparing his body physiologically to fight. Much of the blood flow to his brain has been diverted to strengthen his muscles and heighten his senses, reducing his ability to think rationally. In mind and body, he is transforming into a primitive human animal whose very survival is perceived to be in imminent danger.

CYCLE BREATHING

But, because of your training, you understand that adrenaline in one adversary activates the adrenaline in the other, and you feel your body responding naturally to his adrenaline by releasing your own into your bloodstream. Your heart accelerates, you feel perspiration and your breathing patterns change. So you employ a technique perfected by the military and law enforcement. It's called "cycle breathing." You consciously breathe in deeply through your nose, counting to four, hold to the count of two, exhale out through your mouth to the count of four and hold to the count of two. Again. And again.

Cycle breathing begins to pay off. It relaxes your body, increases blood flow and essential oxygen to your brain, and counteracts the effects of adrenaline to cloud your own logical thinking. You understand that as adrenaline increases your heart rate, you begin to lose your ability to think creatively, innovatively and thoughtfully. According to Redford Williams (1989), General Adaptation Syndrome (GAS) occurs which can virtually cause total suppression of cortical arousal, in other words, your effective thought process. You must consciously slow your heart rate down. You accomplish this by focusing on your heart region and, on the second or third cycle of your cycle breathing, you slow your count down and at the same time slow your heart rate down. Believe me—this works! There is an additional benefit to practicing cycle breathing and consciously lowering your heart rate. According to Pierce J. Howard, Ph.D., during a sustained period of

GAS when the posterior hypothalamus is active, the performance of the immune system is seriously impaired. Minor results of the stress-related impairment include colds, flu, backaches, tight chest, migraine headaches, tension headaches, allergy outbreaks and skin ailments. More chronic and life-threatening results can include hypertension, ulcers, accident-proneness, addictions, asthma, infertility, colon or bowel disorders, diabetes, kidney disease, rheumatoid arthritis and mental illness. Killers that can result include heart disease, stroke, cancer and suicide. In addition, at the lower levels of aggression, like chronic stress and anxiety, results can be energy depletion, depression, insecurity, impotence or frigidity, apathy, emotional withdrawal, confusion, insomnia, chronic fatigue, helplessness, hopelessness, anxiety, lack of concentration and poor memory.

VISUALIZATION AND THE SPLIT-SECOND PAUSE

Every behavior begins with a thought. (The notion that the mind serves as a kind of gatekeeper for emotional or aggressive behavior is at the core of the cognitive theory of emotions. This appraisal activity is typically rapid. It may have several components and may be sequential or simultaneous, but researchers agree that it takes place between stimulus and response. Adapted from Pierce J. Howard, Ph.D., [2001] *The Owner's Manual for the Brain, Everyday Applications from Mind-Brain Research, Second Edition.*) The question is, will this be a constructive thought or a destructive thought? We can plant a constructive thought through visualization; military, law enforcement and professional athletes use this as an effective tool. They call it developing a "conditioned response." The key to this visual exercise is: You win!

As your mind attempts to find a solution to a problem, it will gravitate toward a solution where you received the most emotional pleasure. If you have visually implanted a response to emerging aggression, when and if that particular aggression occurs, you will be mentally prepared for it. This is referred to in the military as *stress inoculation*. Now, while you are calm, you consider all possible opportunities for aggression, and the most effective and professional responses, and you visually implant them in your psyche. For those circumstances where you cannot anticipate a response, the *split-second pause* will give you time to consider what's happening so you can respond both effectively and professionally. Because you take this *split-second pause*, you do respond effectively and professionally—and you win! Now that you have developed a number of effective responses to aggression, wouldn't it be a good idea to sit down with the person you report to and ask their opinion? This person should have a broader picture and experience to enhance possible solutions. While you have this person agreeing with your responses, wouldn't it also be a good idea to have this person sign this document that the two of you have agreed to? Why? This signed document becomes part of your local standard operating procedures, which could compel your organization into backing you in the case of a lawsuit filed against you for responding in this prescribed manner. With signed response in hand, you can now visualize this response with full confidence that, if this kind of aggression should occur and you respond as prescribed, you win!

ACCELERATED AGGRESSION MANAGEMENT

Aggression is occurring right before your eyes. What should be going through your head? First you should be assessing the aggressor. Where is he on the Aggression Continuum? Is he already through the Crisis Phase? Can you still persuade him away from a physical assault or do you need to consider removing yourself and others as a target? Aggressors tend to go through a thought process as they accelerate toward a physical altercation:

- They try to justify their actions
- They consider their alternatives
- They consider the consequences
- They consider their ability to perpetrate the assault

Your objective will be to counter the aggressor's progress toward launching a physical assault. You must illustrate that there is no justification for a physical assault; that there are a number of alternatives to resolve his issues without the use of force; and that the consequences of a physical assault are so horrible that they are unthinkable. Meanwhile you must use non-verbal (manual) pacing to move him away from his ability to perpetrate this act of aggression.

What history do you have on this aggressor? Have you worked with him as an Exploder, a Sherman Tank, etc.? You may have some special skills that you have applied before and that can be applied now.

What is his emotional state? Aggressors tend to experience a domino effect on their emotions: they lose their confidence, then their identity, their self-esteem, and finally, just before they pull the trigger, they lose their dignity. What happens if an aggressor has just done something undignified? Where is he going from here? You may need to re-install the aggressor's dignity so that he regains enough quality of judgment that you will then be able to persuade him further from an act of aggression.

How can you reinstall the aggressor's dignity? Refer back to chapter 6, "Pacing the Aggressor" and review *Reframing*. It suggests a more positive or more honorable motive for an individual to have acted aggressively. *"Bruto, maybe the real reason you've acted this way is that your own standards of quality were frustrated by the rush we've been working under."* In order to establish calm and to dramatize a point, first lower your volume, and then speak with clear, crisp words conveying confidence and competence. Use persuasive pauses for emphasis, effect and mood.

What about the clothes you're wearing? If you anticipate that this escalating aggressor is going to attack, you should consider what you've got on. If you're wearing a tie, a scarf, an identification card lanyard or anything securely around your neck, it can be used to strangle you. He can even grab your earrings to give himself an upper hand. A tight dress and high heels can reduce your mobility. You should be aware that removing items of clothing in front of the aggressor can be a signal to him that you are preparing to fight. It is always better to anticipate this escalation and remove these items in private or at least unobtrusively.

Check the palms of his hands for a weapon, and especially his eyes, which have begun "target glancing" on your mid-section and that vertical lifeline of vital organs a wild animal will rip from his prey in a first strike.

REMOVING YOURSELF AS A TARGET
AND THE "OH GOD!" REFLEX

Then, seemingly in the instant before he lunges around or over the piece of furniture, you divert his attention for just a second or two. You pick up a small object off a nearby desk—not a letter opener but perhaps a handful of paperclips, coins in your pocket or a glass of water you've earlier requested—and hurl it at his face. Our objective is not to injure the aggressor but to throw him into the "Oh God!" reflex, which triggers shock and surprise. This action buys you a half-second or up to a second-and-a-half, to remove yourself as a target. You break to run toward the open door, just beyond which those waiting associates are poised to subdue him, without a blow, without injury.

Much of our ability to remove ourselves as a target is predicated on the "Oh God!" reflex. To understand this reflex, let's discuss that most primal of hormones, adrenaline, as it relates to aggression. The term *aggression* covers everything from the point where an individual feels threatened and is not coping with their anxiety through its ultimate expression, violence. (A potential aggressor channels his appraisal into some form of coping—from the Middle French *couper*; to strike or cut. The strength of the reaction is a direct function of the value of the threat and the degree of certainty that the threat will thwart an objective or a goal. Adapted from Pierce J. Howard, Ph.D., *The Owner's Manual for the Brain, Everyday Applications from Mind-Brain Research.*) You will read, in the pages that follow, many references to the word *threat*. It is the feeling of being threatened and the ability to cope with that threat which denotes the initiation of aggression. The common thread throughout this process is the release of adrenaline.

Lt. Col. Dave Grossman and Bruce Siddle (the authors of "Psychological Effects of Combat," in *Encyclopedia of Violence, Peace and Conflict*) have been conducting landmark studies in the area of adrenaline (or epinephrine) and violence. Dr. Archibald D. Hart (the author of *Adrenaline and Stress, The Exciting New Breakthrough that Helps You Overcome Stress Damage*) has also conducted significant work relating adrenaline to stress. Both Grossman/Siddle and Hart allude to each other's work, but they do not complete the connection between adrenaline (epinephrine) production, stress and violence. To do that, I

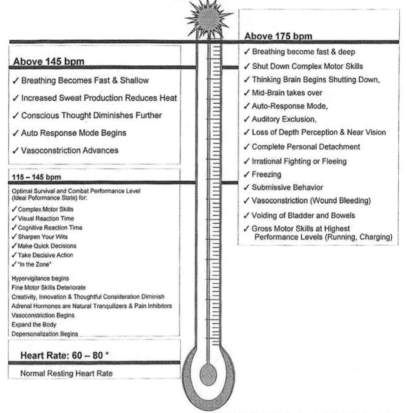

Managing Your Adrenaline

Above 145 bpm

✓ Breathing Becomes Fast & Shallow

✓ Increased Sweat Production Reduces Heat

✓ Conscious Thought Diminishes Further

✓ Auto Response Mode Begins

✓ Vasoconstriction Advances

115 – 145 bpm

Optimal Survival and Combat Performance Level
(Ideal Peformance State) for:

✓ Complex Motor Skills
✓ Visual Reaction Time
✓ Cognitive Reaction Time
✓ Sharpen Your Wits
✓ Make Quick Decisions
✓ Take Decisive Action
✓ "In the Zone"

Hypervigilance begins
Fine Motor Skills Deteriorate
Creativity, Innovation & Thoughtful Consideration Diminish
Adrenal Hormones are Natural Tranquilizers & Pain Inhibitors
Vasoconstriction Begins
Expand the Body
Depersonalization Begins

Heart Rate: 60 – 80 *

Normal Resting Heart Rate

Above 175 bpm

✓ Breathing become fast & deep

✓ Shut Down Complex Motor Skills

✓ Thinking Brain Begins Shutting Down,

✓ Mid-Brain takes over

✓ Auto-Response Mode,

✓ Auditory Exclusion,

✓ Loss of Depth Perception & Near Vision

✓ Complete Personal Detachment

✓ Irrational Fighting or Fleeing

✓ Freezing

✓ Submissive Behavior

✓ Vasoconstriction (Wound Bleeding)

✓ Voiding of Bladder and Bowels

✓ Gross Motor Skills at Highest
Performance Levels (Running, Charging)

* Heart Rate (bpm) can vary from one individual to another

Figure 8.2   *Illustration of Adrenaline on Heart Rate (Adapted from Lt. Col. Dave Grossman and Bruce Siddle, "Psychological Effects of Combat," in* Encyclopedia of Violence, Peace and Conflict*)*

created the Primal Aggression Continuum. Figure 8.2, "Managing Your Adrenaline," illustrates aggression's adrenaline rush from its genesis (stress) through its ultimate result (violence). It measures the effects of emerging adrenaline on heart rate and "non-verbal leakage," or behavior and body language; and on the verbal aggression scale that it produces both in an aggressor and in ourselves.

We can use the Primal Aggression Continuum, which is based on the research and findings of Grossman, Siddle and Hart, to track an aggressor's escalation. From a resting heart rate of approximately 60–80 beats per minute (bpm) to about 115–145 bpm, then above 145 bpm, into the range exceeding 175 bpm, an aggressor is on the verge of losing physical control and is about to attack. At this level the aggressor is only able to process one thing at a time in a period of half-a-second to a second-and-a-half. In other words, if you confront an aggressor with more then one thing during this split second, he will not be able to cope. He will go into the "Oh God!" reflex.

Here's an excellent illustration. An aggressor at the heart rate level above 175 bpm confronts you. If the aggressor were at a lesser level you would still be talking to him, using your verbal and non-verbal persuasion skills. You look over his shoulder and yell, "grab him!" The aggressor will immediately go into to the "Oh God!" reflex, spinning around to deal with a perceived attacker. This should give you that precious split second to rush around his other side and remove yourself as a target.

We find that aggression and violence often erupt in direct proportion to the way a *victim* responds to an aggressor. When you have an aggressor before you whose adrenaline is already surging, it is a natural human response for your adrenaline to surge, preparing you for attack. What are you going to do with your adrenaline? In the absence of any adrenaline control, you as the "victim" may well trigger an escalation of aggression, forcing this into a showdown and perhaps a physical assault. As we consider managing adrenaline in ourselves, we can draw from the methods used by the military and now by many in the law enforcement community. There are three methods of managing adrenaline.

MEASURING AND MANAGING OUR EMOTIONS—A BREAKTHROUGH!

As we've seen, this technique controls not just your breathing, but your adrenaline. And by controlling the fuel to aggression, your adrenaline, you're able to manage emotions and anger. In the business world, we understand that in order to effectively *manage* a program or situation, we must be able to *measure* it, so that we have a yardstick of our effectiveness. Until now, we had no such yardstick to measure anger. Now, as we've seen above, we have the Primal Aggression Continuum to *measure* that aggression. And through cycle breathing, we also have the means to *manage* it, at least in ourselves.

Stress Inoculation

The military has used this technique for years. When a soldier is forced to crawl along the ground with live rounds being fired just above him, he is being trained through "stress inoculation" for the time when real bullets will be flying. Thus having been "inoculated," the soldier won't go into the "Oh God!" reflex when the first bullet zings past him.

Commercial airlines spend millions on complex flight simulators, using "stress inoculation" to prepare pilots, in the safe environment of a simulator, for every possible flight emergency. After "experiencing" engine fires, clear air turbulence, loss of air pressure and any number of other stressful situations, pilots are thoroughly inoculated to perform a checklist of procedures calmly and automatically in order to save the aircraft and its passengers.

You can achieve the same effects of stress inoculation by using visualization as described under "Visualization and the Split Second Pause" on page 106.

Conditioned Response

People tend to act a great deal of the time from pre-conditioning. This takes nothing away from our ability to think rationally and make conscious decisions. But a complex, convoluted world constantly barrages us with information—too much information for any reasonable person to assimilate. So we tend, consciously or unconsciously, to create shortcuts. These shortcuts are both a blessing and a curse. We are conditioned by our shortcuts. When a certain situation or circumstance arises, we respond in a certain way. The more often the situation or circumstance occurs, the more automatic our response. Over time, this response is so ingrained in us that it's hard not to respond in a conditioned way. The response has become a habit.

Habits created by shortcuts can be constructive or destructive. Stereotyping of others is a form of shortcut; we make judgments of those in our vicinity based upon our experiences and our knowledge. We can't offer a thorough evaluation of every individual who enters our environment so we make judgments based on shortcut stereotyping. This can be either useful or detrimental based on its application, but stereotyping bias has no place in an aggression moment. As an Aggression Manager it is essential to thoroughly evaluate each emerging aggressor.

The military trains their troops to react with constructive conditioned responses. They practice, practice and practice until they have instilled specific shortcuts, which have become habits that make the soldier respond quickly and effectively—and survive the experience.

In modern military field training, computer simulation has been able to replicate many of the sights and sounds of warfare, in order to prepare troops for actual combat. Prior to the development of computer simulation, the most effective training employed field practice with the use of mental visualization. Even today, troops who have visualized combat, heard the gunfire and smelled the phosphorus in their minds, will know almost instinctively how to perform should they be thrust onto the battlefield.

We can do the same. Using visualization, we can picture possible aggression that can explode into our world and visually practice the most effective and professional response. In this way we become thoroughly prepared, and able to respond to aggression in much the same way as the soldier—quickly, effectively and safely.

So although persuasion in a specific instance may not work—and it happens—you can escape harm by planning ahead, by careful positioning, and by reading the signs of adrenaline in the aggressor. In addition, by feeling the adrenaline surge in yourself and neutralizing its rush to maximize your powers of reason and judgment, you can maintain steady control of a dangerous, deteriorating situation.

The action is over. The danger has passed. But investigations by law enforcement and attorneys may have just begun. Now, using the clarity of immediacy, is the time to sit down and document what has just occurred, with clinical accuracy.

What happens if we get caught alone with an aggressor? I recommend that if you have any idea that there could be physical aggression you should have a team ready to support you. What team? Whether in the workplace or school setting you should have a Crisis Response Team available to you. But what if the aggressor is escalating right in front of you and the Crisis Response Team is not available? Then you have no choice but to implement solo intervention.

SOLO INTERVENTIONS

Solo interventions are designed for you to remove yourself as a target, predicated on the effective use, upon the aggressor, of the "Oh God!" reflex.

It is always, always better to utilize team intervention. If you suspect for one moment that a person could be overtly aggressive with you, it is always better to use a team rather than handle it alone. But for all your precautions, you may still be caught alone. What do you do then?

These solo interventions were derived from Ninjutsu. This is the art used by the Ninjas. I have an interest in the Ninjas' culture because they were not just warriors. They were given very specific tasks and they had to use their heads to complete these tasks. One of these tasks was reconnaissance. They had to infiltrate a hostile area, gather information on the enemy and return without being detected. The methods they used to safely remove themselves as targets are the skills we are going to call upon for our solo interventions.

Before we discuss these interventions, let's set the stage. We are at that point when an aggressor is coming at us very quickly and we have to *respond* . . . not just *react* or we could get into trouble. So take a split-second pause and evaluate what's happening to you and how you are going to respond. Remember, we included the split-second pause in our visualization so that it would be available when you needed it.

Analysis Paralysis

The same brain system, i.e., right brain/left brain, which deals with emotions and generates movement, also deals with decision-making and rational thinking. If we allow ourselves to become too emotional, we will not be able to think rationally. (Focused aggression is accompanied by higher than normal levels of testosterone and is characterized by partially suppressed cortical arousal; therefore, both creativity and problem-solving ability are reduced. Adapted from Redford Williams [1989] *The Trusting Heart: Great News about Type A Behavior*.) If we put too much emphasis on rational thinking or over rationalizing, we won't have the emotions to move our body when we need to. We call this analysis paralysis. We must create a whole body/whole brain synergy that allows us to think clearly and pragmatically as well as move quickly on demand. The best way to achieve the ideal balance is through cycle breathing.

Get Real

We must also get real. We, in the Western world, tend to see violence as something that one gets only on TV or in the movies, not in real life. So when violence does confront us we tend, to some degree, to go into shock. We as Aggression Managers cannot afford to go into shock. We must be there, alert and calm, throughout the experience so that we can effectively remove ourselves as a target and survive the encounter. The only way to achieve this calm objectivity, and be able to maximize our actions in an aggression moment, is to cycle breathe. As we've already learned, cycle breathing is possibly the most important tool for individuals caught in the throes of aggression.

Reactionary Gap

The reactionary gap is the minimum distance that Aggression Managers should maintain between an unarmed aggressor and themselves. It is the distance created when two individuals—the Aggression Manager and the aggressor—extend their arms and touch their extended fingers. This distance requires the aggressor to make two movements to get to the Aggression Manager and perpetrate an attack, providing the Aggression Manager the opportunity of blocking the incoming strike and removing himself or herself as a target. Between two equally capable individuals, no *reaction* is as fast as an *action*, therefore the Aggression Manager must maintain this reactionary gap.

Interview Stance

Like the reactionary gap, the interview stance is taught to virtually all new police academy recruits. It is invaluable when you find yourself close to an escalating aggressor, possibly within the reactionary gap. This offers the Aggression Manager maximum speed, balance and safety without appearing threatening to the aggressor. The stance starts with your feet shoulder-width apart, knees slightly bent. You are standing at a 45-degree angle to the aggressor, with your hands either cupped in front of you or outstretched with palms up in a submissive fashion. This interview stance appears submissive and cooperative but allows you the ability to move quickly to block an incoming strike and remove yourself as a target. Because you are standing at a 45-degree angle to the aggressor, you will be able to, by a quarter turn, remove your lifeline as the target of an attack. Yet the same 45-degree angle lets you get as close as possible to an aggressor without provoking him or causing him to escalate. Standing at a 45-degree angle to the aggressor is called blading. We know that Americans typically like about three feet of distance when standing face-to-face with each other. We like about 18 inches distance when side-to-side, so by standing at a 45-degree angle to the aggressor typically we can get closer, maintain eye contact and not provoke or escalate the aggressor.

Now let's examine the specific methods of solo intervention.

The Angle Method

This method is predicated on what happens to an aggressor's peripheral vision when his adrenaline level is above 175 bpm. His focus is narrowed to that thin-lined area we refer to as the lifeline. In other words, his angle of peripheral vision has narrowed almost to 0 degrees. This becomes your advantage. You have your hands, as in the interview Stance, outreached with palms up. The aggressor sees you as submissive and non-threatening. Yet the aggressor does not actually see your hands. When the aggressor rears back to start his strike you move forward, and use the heel of your palm to push him off balance and back. He goes into the "Oh God!" reflex, giving you the opportunity of passing right by him, removing yourself as a target.

The Blinding Method

This method is predicated on an old Chinese proverb: A grain of sand in the eye can hide a mountain. Remember that our objective with each of these methods is to use the "Oh God!" reflex. If you have an aggressor at 175-bpm heart rate caused by adrenaline, any movement toward his eyes will throw him into the "Oh God!" reflex. Use coins in your pocket or purse, water or non-toxic substances. Remember all you're trying to do is escape. So don't use hot coffee, pencils or a lead ashtray. Your objective is not to injure him but remove yourself as a target.

The Misdirection Method

This strategy is simple. We are trying to give the impression that we're going one direction, while in fact we're going in another. The Ninjas love misdirection techniques. You have an aggressor bearing down on you. Look over his shoulder and yell "Grab him." The aggressor instinctively spins around to deal with what he perceives as an attack from the rear, throwing him into the "Oh God!" reflex. So you pivot around the opposite side and remove yourself as a target.

The Scarf Method

This method borrows a technique from magicians who drape a scarf over a cage, with a dove inside . . . Abracadabra . . . and the dove is gone! The magician uses a technique the Ninjas loved: illusion. You can use this method of illusion to protect yourself. How? By hiring a plainclothes police officer or security person sitting outside your office door. The aggressor will believe that this is just another individual waiting for an appointment—not a trained professional prepared to take control at a moments notice.

The Mind Method

Ninjas loved knowledge. They believed knowledge was power. Others around them thought the Ninjas were magical, achieving seemingly impossible physical feats with relative ease. What these observers did not know was that the Ninjas not only loved knowledge, but achieved higher levels of knowledge through continuously practicing what they learned until it became second nature. Much of that knowledge was about themselves and of what they could accomplish with a harmony of mind and body. Today, thanks to the impact of *Star Wars*, we might equate this with "The Force."

By reading this book you are acquiring the basic knowledge about Aggression Management. But now you must practice, practice and practice until these skills become second nature to you . . . until people around you say, "I didn't think anybody could do that, but you did it and made it look easy!"

TEAM INTERVENTION VERSUS SOLO INTERVENTION

I recommend team intervention for three reasons:

1. You have the advantage of safety in numbers. One more person can make the aggression situation twice as safe.
2. It promotes professionalism. A team looks more professional and an aggressor is more likely to respond constructively if a professional looking team approaches him.
3. A team will support you in the event of litigation. What do your team members become? Built-in witnesses. Whose witnesses are they? Yours!

Who Should Be the Leader?

Sometimes the leader is pre-determined by company protocol. In the absences of this protocol, what qualities are you looking for?

- The first Aggression Manager on the scene. You want someone with Aggression Management skills.
- You want someone with confidence—not cocky, but with a demeanor of quiet confidence that undermines aggressive behavior.
- Who has the most knowledge of the aggressor? Have you ever

worked with the aggressor as a Sherman Tank, an Exploder, etc.? You may have a special relationship and skills to be applied.

HOW DOES A ROBBERY DIFFER?

Whether you work in an environment where you might be robbed, or find yourself in a local convenience store that is being robbed, it is wise to understand the principles of a robbery. The mission of a robber differs from other aggressors. He sees himself as a farmer and you as his harvest. It is really that simple. Robbers get very indignant when you don't let them rob you.

Is there anything you own worth losing your life over? I hope not. We recommend that you cooperate, and get others to cooperate too. Your life may depend on how you get others to cooperate. Give the robber what he wants and get him out of there. Also, let the robber leave the premises. Why? If law enforcement arrives and the robber is still in with you, what do you become? That's right, a hostage!

Ten percent of all armed robberies end in murder. What does this mean to you? Ninety percent don't. Let the robber have what he wants and don't become a statistic. If you have just been robbed and the robber now wants you to get in his car, don't! Statistics are against you. There are only three reasons why they want to take you somewhere else, more secluded. They want to rape you, torture you and/or murder you. How do you avoid going? Remember the robber is not thinking rationally, so you can use what are called "disconcerts." These are phrases that can disrupt the thought process of the robber. Some examples that have worked are: (convenience store) "There are three undercover detectives who come here at this time every day for coffee. You better take this money and get out of here fast!"; "I'm the manager here, so I can't leave"; and one manager faked a faint. The robbers were not going to drag her into the car so it worked!

Finally, you must observe, observe, observe. Even though the predator may be wearing a mask, you can observe his body language, his posture, even the direction that he turns as he exits the door. Have you ever noticed numbers printed on the inside left door frame in many convenience stores? They're there to help determine the height of a robber as he leaves the premises. Whether these numbers exist at the location of your encounter or not, you can identify any mark on the wall next to the door as a point of reference for the height of a robber which can be measured later.

PREDATOR'S INTERVIEW

Predators do not want difficult prey. They want easy prey. Do you look like easy prey? Predators pay careful attention to the body language of prospective prey and are instantly "attracted" to potential victims. Once the predator has identified you as his prey he will attempt to catch you off guard. He sizes you up in seconds through your:

- Voice
- Eye movements
- Muscle tension
- Breathing and posture
- The way you hold your belongings

How do they catch you off guard? The predator makes up lies and stories to distract you, such as asking you for money, the time or directions.

The Predator's Stare

This is the aggressor's holding mechanism. Its purpose is to demonstrate power over his victim. The objective is to get and hold the victim's attention, like a snake mesmerizes its prey before the attack. The aggressor's purpose is to evoke an emotional response, namely *fear*. Typically, this may be your last chance to avoid attack. Follow the predator's stare, and in the absence of anything to the contrary the predator will carry out his attack.

I am often asked about eye contact with a possible aggressor. Every situation is unique and should be considered separately. Generally, we find that if you are walking along a street where there are individuals who concern you, change direction and remove yourself as a possible target. If this isn't possible, walk through these individuals as if they were trees in a forest. You see the trees, you walk around the trees but you will not look directly at the trees.

This brings to mind an old adage: "Never look where you don't want to go." It is also important to walk with a purpose, as if you know where you're going and are not being deterred. If you feel it is appropriate, it may be helpful to acknowledge these individuals by giving them a short and directed nod of your head, to show respect.

If an individual steps out in front of you and blocks your way, the most effective response may be to look back at them with a detached look. (Remember: without saying a word, your look of detachment says to that attacker "I'm not going to be easy!") and then say something in passing like "Good afternoon." You aren't looking for an answer. This will be only a glancing encounter because you aren't stopping for a chat. You continue through the area as you step around and continue down the street.

DOMESTIC VIOLENCE SPILL OVER

There were some 13,000 attacks on women in the workplace by husbands or boyfriends during a recent12-month period! This is no longer just a domestic problem. It is spilling over into the workplace. We must become more aware and more responsive to this issue.

How? If an employee comes to work with physical injuries, tactfully inquire as to how she came to have these injuries. Once you have identified what happened to her, begin assisting her in getting the help she needs.

How can you become more aware? A co-worker or staff member may appear quiet, withdrawn or isolated, often late or even absent from work. If she starts to shows signs of emotional distress or depression, these are the same signs of Mounting Anxiety in our Aggression Continuum. You should approach this person, find out the situation and offer your help. How about a co-worker regularly receiving gifts or flowers? You approach her and say "Nice flowers. What's the occasion?" If she says something like, "He's making up for the other night," maybe you should ask more questions!

Why is it in your best interest to do this? Not only does this person deserve your attention but if an aggressor comes into the workplace looking for his target and you inadvertently get in the way, you too can become a target.

In most states citizens can get a restraining order legally preventing an aggressor from approaching their home. But it is almost impossible to get a restraining order keeping an aggressor away from your workplace without your employer's permission. If you're a manager, we suggest you look into these rules and how they apply in your state. Consider helping these employees get legal protection, and consider developing policies and procedures to protect them. Stalking laws differ from state to state and some states offer victim's advocates to help protect victims of domestic abuse. Look into what can be done and decide to do it, remember—anyone who *permits* themselves to be battered goes way beyond our ability as an Aggression Manager to help them. Refer them to an employee assistance program or other professional counselor.

ROAD RAGE

One recent hot summer in Los Angeles, the freeways became a virtual shooting gallery as drivers repeatedly lost their temper. Meanwhile, two drivers in Orlando got into a road rage incident and pulled off the road to settle it with words. Then one driver, an otherwise decent family man, walked back to his car, pulled out a baseball bat, and bashed in the skull of the other driver's wife.

The term "road rage" has become fashionable because of the seeming growing number of such incidents. Yet I often wonder how so many of these incidents occur. The fact is that road rage may be one of the easier aggression moments to defuse. How? By removing yourself as a target. Don't engage!

We humans seem to have the need to face our aggressor. You know what I mean. You are driving along merrily and someone cuts in front of you. It bothers you. You know that you should let this person go about his way but you want to know who could do this to you? You aren't angered . . . you just want to see their face. This is a very dangerous curiosity and this is how we begin our engagement with the enemy.

They respond with a vulgar gesture and you escalate. Don't engage! *Don't fall into the trap of having to see the face of your aggressor.* It used to be that both parties made their vulgar gesture and then went about their way, but now they pull out their 9 mm handgun and war begins.

The Aggression Continuum for Road Rage

Trigger Phase:

- Honking at someone
- Giving an offensive hand gesture
- Yelling at someone or swearing
- Revving your engine to indicate displeasure
- Shining your high beams in retaliation
- Deliberately cutting someone off
- Tailgating
- Braking suddenly to punish a tailgater
- Blocking a line
- Racing

Escalation Phase:

- Verbal road rage
- Yelling, cursing, honking, name-calling
- Non-verbal road rage
- Gesturing, complaining to yourself, rushing, competing, resisting

Crisis Phase:

- Cutting off, blocking, chasing, fighting, shooting

Where is this coming from? We are told that there are more cars and less space. We are told that disrespect and even rage have become cultural norms. We seem to need to race to our destination at a maximum rate of speed and we are often motivated by righteous indignation, or by the impulse to deal vigilante justice to road rage perpetrators. "You moron! You just cut me off, so now I'm going to cut you off. See how you like it!" The problem nowadays is that your road nemesis of the moment may have a gun under his seat and may decide to use it.

Road Rage, Recovery

Defensive driving takes us a long way toward diminishing this problem. If you are thinking ahead, if you expect the worst, you're not shocked and enraged when others take inappropriate action against you. This helps you not go through the "Oh God!" reflex. Then we suggest that you drive constructively:

- Act tolerant, be forgiving, be helpful
- Reframe your picture. If someone cuts you off, consider he may have had an emergency and he must get to the hospital emergency room.
- Consider that the other driver may suffer from reduced mental capacity, and is not worth the energy it takes to get mad at him.
- Take a deep breath. Begin cycle breathing. Maintain your calm.

THE ART OF MANUAL PERSUASION

There is indeed a fourth art not reflected in the chapter titles. It is predicated on the following circumstances: You are cornered by an aggressor, and being prepared is not enough. Your verbal and non-verbal persuasion is not enough, and your attempts to escape are non-existent. You've got a serious problem.

What are you going to do? There are only two options available. Collapse and become a victim, or *fight* your way out! Although some will collapse and become victims, if you ask a roomful of people how many will fight their way out, virtually every person in the room will raise his hand. Every man, that is, and even most women.

With that said, we've already taken the position that fighting is not an option. Instead, we recommend the alternative to fighting, the Art of Manual Persuasion.

The Art of Manual Persuasion is the "art" of last resort. It involves techniques used to take control of an aggressor without injuring the individual. No injury, no *basis* for a lawsuit. Notice that I did not say "no lawsuit." Manual persuasion uses pain to induce compliance. This is not the kind of pain where you would take an aspirin. This is reflex pain. You evoke these techniques and the aggressor's reflex impulses causes him to comply. The beauty of reflex pain is that the bigger and stronger the aggressor the quicker and greater the pain. In this way a 120-pound woman can manually persuade a 240-pound aggressor with a smile on her face and a grimace on his. No matter what your size or athletic condition, these techniques can work for you.

This is not martial arts, wrestling, boxing, nor striking in any way. It is *physiological engineering,* or engineering the body to create and manage the aggressor's reflex pain. We teach two concepts: wrist compliance and finger compliance, and from these simple concepts we have developed over 60 effective techniques. But remember—no techniques work all the time on every individual; and these techniques require a skill level that demands regular practice.

You should resort to manual persuasion only when *being prepared, persuasion* and *safe escape* are no longer viable options. At the same time you must also remember that you are responsible for your actions. As we have already stated, when it comes to reasonable force, no matter what you do, someone—an attorney, a judge—is likely to ask very serious questions, and you had better have very good answers. You must be very circumspect about your action and be ready to document every aspect of the actions of the aggressor together with your own actions.

I'm often asked, "But what if one of my employees uses these techniques prematurely?" The answer is, we do not live in a litigation free world. You can do nothing and still be sued. The most important question must be, "are these actions defensible?" Can you defend yourself against a lawsuit if someone uses these skills prematurely? Throughout the Art of Manual Persuasion workshop we ask the participants "When do you use these manual persuasion skills?" And, in unison, everyone proclaims "only as a last resort." There will be plenty of witnesses that will concur that these skills are to be used "only as a last resort." Finally, when the employer has an employee placed in the above circumstances, what will they do? Will they fight their way out? If they do *fight*, the legal action that will surely follow may be far more injurious.

The techniques of the Art of Manual Persuasion require live demonstration and training, and cannot be taught effectively in this book. Therefore, only the Center for Aggression Management certified master instructors teach this "art." Should you desire more information regarding the Art of Manual Persuasion, please contact the Center for Aggression Management at 1-800-260-7231 in Winter Park, FL.

THE ARTS OF AGGRESSION MANAGEMENT

Let's conclude our discussion on Aggression Management skills themselves and summarize their application in various settings.

Have you noticed how certain people can walk into a room and the bad guys leave them alone and the good guys are drawn to them. We believe these individuals have a *persona of certainty*. Does this mean that they have all the answers in this uncertain world? Of course not. What this means is that they have skills with which they are confident and, although they'll make mistakes, they know that they can and will work through their errors.

Over the Aggression Management journey we have taken, we have shared with you the three Arts of Aggression Management and introduced you to a fourth, the Art of Manual Persuasion. Each "art" is inescapably connected with the others. When you're considering the Art of Safe Escape, have you forgotten about the Art of Being Prepared? Of course not. When you're in Safe Escape have you forgotten using the Art of Persuasion? Of course not. While you're considering the Art of Being Prepared, are you considering the Art of Safe Escape? I hope so. Each art is inexorably connected under the umbrella of the Arts of Aggression Management. Why are they called the "arts?" We may use techniques that are based in science but how well we apply these techniques will be an art. So practice these techniques and make the Arts of Aggression Management an art form for you.

We at the center believe that for every incident, there are always pre-incidents. The question is, will you identify them? You must be alert and utilize these Aggression Management skills to identify them, so that you can foresee the possibility of conflict. Foreseeing this conflict will cause you the sense of urgency and responsibility to engage and prevent aggression in the first place. Although, we have also offered Aggression Management skills to engage an aggressor who needs intervention, our primary focus is on how to prevent aggression in the first place. This is the primary objective of an Aggression Manager.

CHAPTER 9

Managing to Protect Our Kids in School

by Dr. Dennis J. Kowalski, Superintendent, Strongsville City Schools, Strongsville, Ohio

Moses Lake, Washington—Barry Loukaitis, 14, shoots and kills a teacher and two students at Frontier Junior High, after being teased by school athletes.

Pearl, Mississippi—Luke Woodham, 16, kills two students and wounds seven at Pearl High School, after his girlfriend called him pudgy and gay.

Jonesboro, Arkansas—Andrew Goldman, 11, and Mitchell Johnson, 13, shoot and kill a teacher and four students, and wound ten more, using three rifles and seven handguns. They had both been rejected by girls; Johnson was teased for being fat.

Santee, California, Santana High School—Andy Williams, 17, shot and killed 2 and wounded 13 more.

Littleton, Colorado—We all know the story of Columbine High School.

As an educator for the past 33 years and an administrator for 28 of those years, I have seen and dealt with aggression in students, staff members, parents and other members of the community.

I have taken weapons from students and estranged spouses of staff members. I have broken up fights between students, between students and teachers, between staff members and even between staff members and parents. I have tried to defuse aggressive behavior in a variety of circumstances among students, staff members and parents.

Reflecting on how I dealt with aggression I've often wondered whether or not I was acting properly in trying to reduce it, and have worried that I might have even made the aggression worse. Did I simply stop the aggression for that moment only to have the aggressor display hostility later and/or in another setting? Why didn't I predict the aggression?

Over the years, I have also observed other staff members respond to aggressive incidents, and have in fact seen staff members incite more aggression rather than defuse it.

I recall vividly an assistant principal arguing with a student. I knew that the student was a high-strung kid who angered easily. I cringed as the assistant principal kept badgering the youngster until the boy shouted for the assistant principal to "F——— off!" and ran from the office. When I confronted my colleague about this incident, I explained to him how he had pushed the student beyond his limit of tolerance and only made the situation worse.

However, I was discouraged at his lack of knowledge and skills in recognizing aggression, and his inability to control and adjust his behavior to avoid escalating the student's aggression.

I recall a six-foot-three basketball coach reprimanding a much smaller eighth-grade student, standing three inches from the student and poking his finger in the boy's chest. This provoked the student into eventually getting arrested because of his angry response.

A sixth-grade boy told a classmate he was going to shoot him. The parents of the threatened student immediately transferred their son from the school. The parents of other children soon demanded that the student be relocated from their school.

On another occasion, I dealt with a troubled youngster who we eventually suspended from school for misbehavior. His parents were apparently very strict, so the boy got very little understanding or support from home. He committed suicide. Why didn't we read the signs?

Still another time, an emotionally handicapped student refused to leave the classroom. Staff members confronted the angry student, who verbally threatened them and physically fought his way out of the classroom. Police were called to forcibly restrain the boy. His parents immediately filed suit.

The lack of skill in identifying and defusing aggression has been a concern of mine for years. I have seen many incidents in which the school employee—a teacher, principal, custodian, playground aide or secretary—didn't have a clue about what to do with an aggressive situation and in fact inadvertently escalated the level of aggression.

As superintendent of an affluent suburban school district, I was confronted by many parents on the day after the Columbine incident, all-asking, "Dr. K., what are you doing about violence at *our* school?"

A popular local radio station talk show reported that my district was just like Columbine. He and his callers alike suggested it could have happened in my district. And, in fact, our actual demographics are very similar to those of Columbine.

In response, we immediately increased our security by adding a hotline, by stationing a greeter in the high school, and requiring employee's identification badges. We also added video monitors at entry points of selected elementary schools, began locking all doors except one for entry after the school day had begun—and performing the "infamous" security assessment.

Those actions all gave me a response to questions about "what were we doing," but they were really just surface stuff. The Columbine incident, along with the other school tragedies, has reinforced the need to have staff members understand and apply new levels of knowledge and skills regarding aggression.

School personnel see aggression in students and colleagues on a regular basis. Whether they're verbal comments, physical confrontation, or changes in behavior, these forms of aggression are warning signs that need to be detected and dealt with. The U.S. Secret Service, in their Safe School Initiative Report in October 2000, told us: "There is no accurate or useful profile of the school shooter, nor for assessing the risk that a particular student may pose for school-based targeted violence." I believe this also applies to staff. The report went on to say, "An inquiry should focus instead on a student's behaviors and communications" to determine if the student appears to be planning or preparing for an attack. This is where Aggression Management applies.

I believe that Aggression Management training would help school personnel identify aggression among students and other staff members, and give them the skills to reduce this aggression. Aggression Management would also give us all a yardstick with which to assess our own behavior, and make us more vigilant of our individual responses to aggressive incidents.

As we learn from Dr. Byrnes, when there is an aggressor, whose adrenaline is already pumping, it is a natural human response for your adrenaline to rise preparing you for an attack. All too often this adrenaline serves to escalate an already bad situation. Many times a situation could have been de-escalated if it were not for the victim's adrenaline taking over, causing that individual to respond in a way that exacerbates the problem. Dr. Byrnes has developed a method of measuring aggression, and thereby managing it in others and in us, thus providing the means to prevent aggression before conflict occurs.

In the state of Ohio, where I have spent my career, Ohio Revise Code requires new teachers to complete a six-hour training course on child abuse recognition. Given the alarming growth of aggression in our schools, it seems just as crucial, in the interest of the safety of *everyone* in the school environment, to provide training in Aggression Management.

I teach as an adjunct professor at several local universities. One of my favorite courses is Psychology of Teaching and Learning, a graduate-level course. I marvel at students' lack of knowledge in the areas of dealing with disruptive students and with student motivation. Aggression Management would be a welcome component to the college coursework for educators both at the undergraduate and graduate level.

In inner city schools, teachers are faced with students that come to school with a lot of unfortunate baggage—youngsters from poverty-ridden, drug-invested, high crime neighborhoods. Dr. James Garbarino (1999) refers to these students as "socially toxic." Their aggression may be a response to the perceived hopelessness they feel about their lives. Aggression Management for urban school educators would likely enable these teachers to help kids cope as well as give them skills to improve their self-image.

Aggression Management training will provide the classroom teacher with a variety of identification skills as noted:

- Importance of knowledge of Aggression Continuum especially the "trigger." This is a workshop in itself for all staff.
- Reframing—reference to the baggage that kids come to school

with: divorce or other family/social problems; socially toxic kids (Garbarino).

- Paraphrasing as a tool to persuade a student away from aggression.
- Probing questions used to pace students away from aggression.
- Non-verbal cues that can cause the escalation of aggression— Teachers traditionally stand over a student in conflict—this heightens the emotion of a student. Teachers should sit down so that both parties are at the same plane.
- Application of the split second pause.
- The need to have skill to assess the aggressor.
- Reaction versus prevention.
- Road rage tips should be part of driver ed. prep.

My recommendations for Aggression Management go beyond the classroom and the office. I believe Aggression Management should be used with all staff members. Secretaries, bus drivers, custodians, and playground staff constantly interact with students. They need to be able to identify signs that would ultimately prevent larger scale aggression.

With Aggression Management training our school staff will have tools to avoid some of the horrific tragedies that have plagued our school buildings.

CHAPTER 10

How to Prevent Aggression in Healthcare

There Are More Non-Fatal Attacks in Healthcare and Social Services than Any Other Industry

by Dennis Jones, RN, MS

There is a reason why the U.S. Department of Labor's Occupational Safety and Health Administration (OSHA) wrote the *Guidelines for Preventing Workplace Violence for Health Care and Social Service Workers* in 1996. There is a reason why California passed legislation in 1993 that provided severe punishment for acts of violence against healthcare workers, and required employers to provide training in prevention. There is a reason why the American Academy of Nurses hosted a national conference on violence to identify research priorities and make policy recommendations. And there is a reason why a coalition of healthcare worker labor unions was formed to bring the problem of violence to the attention of OSHA, and lobby for a standard to prevent violence in the workplace. This led to the OSHA guidelines mentioned above.

The majority of the literature published in both the recent past and today uses the term "workplace violence" to characterize the various forms of verbal, emotional and physical abuse committed by one human being against another in the workplace setting. And, depending on the individual and his or her own life experiences, the term "violence" may conjure up any number of extreme situations or negative experiences. Therefore, violence may have as many definitions as there are people to experience it.

Seldom, if ever, is aggression referenced as an overall acceptable term to define the acts above. This author defines violence as "aggression—expressed" or the "expression of aggression." That expression can take on a much broader variety of forms, e.g., yelling or screaming, use of derogatory names, aggressive eye contact, intimidating verbal or physical actions, verbal or physical threats, and finally, harmful physical contact. The multitude of ways in which aggression is expressed or manifested (violence) in the healthcare setting, and ways to manage it, is what this chapter attempts to address. Therefore, whenever the term "violence" is used, the reader is encouraged to begin to mentally define and envision it as the "expression of aggression" regardless of its form.

It is clear that healthcare providers are at increased risk for becoming victims of violence in their workplace. In fact, according to the U.S. Bureau of Justice Statistics, nurses are victims of non-fatal assault at a rate of 24.9 per thousand, much higher than the average of 14.8 per thousand for all occupations. There are many reasons for this and they vary as much as the variety of settings wherein healthcare workers practice their craft. In the acute hospital setting the hotbeds for individuals with overly aggressive tendencies are the Emergency (ED) and Psychiatric departments. The ED is the window to the community served by the hospital and in almost all instances there is an open door policy. This allows almost anyone to enter the ED area (waiting room, registration and triage nurse) without challenge. Those EDs located in urban settings where there is an increased incidence of violent crimes are at particular risk. This is especially true if the ED serves as the trauma center for the community, particularly since it is not uncommon for a trauma center to receive both the victim *and* the perpetrator of a violent crime. However, even if the ED is not a trauma center, there is still risk due to the presence of individuals engaging in substance abuse that, for a multitude of reasons, find themselves in the ED setting.

For some, just *being* in the ED, either as a patient or visitor/family member is stressful and leads to an increase in anxiety, which may express itself in the form of violence toward a healthcare worker, depending on how it is managed. A prolonged wait in an ED waiting room that is perceived as unnecessary *and* placing a loved one at risk, is a commonplace situation which, if not handled carefully, can become particularly volatile. Frequently, the frontline staff personnel who are most commonly responsible for addressing such situations are nurses, who often are without the support of security or some other form of authoritative presence. This results in the nursing staff serving as first-line security. Obviously, staff in this role are at tremendous risk of physical injury, and in the worst-case scenario, workplace death.

Although inpatient psychiatric units are at great risk for the presence of aggression in their patient population, they have been, historically, the best prepared to manage the aggressive client. Besides mandatory Aggression Management educational programs for psychiatric staff members, the physical design of the units often allows for better management of the potentially violent patient. Examples include the following: control of access and egress to and from the unit through the use of locked doors, specially designed seclusion rooms for isolation of the violent individual from staff and other patients to allow for controlled de-escalation, and a limited presence of unnecessary medical equipment that could be used as weapons (IV pole, needles, etc.). In some cases, closed circuit monitoring of the unit is employed with a consistent security presence for safety. Unfortunately, other areas of the hospital are not as well monitored or safe in the event a violent incident occurs.

As was previously mentioned, guidelines exist for healthcare organizations for the *prevention* of violence in the workplace. However, many organizations have failed to employ such measures. Instead, the focus is on resolving conflict at the time of its occurrence. As you have heard, conflict resolution *pre-supposes* conflict. Our opinion is, if you wait for conflict to occur, you have waited too long! You have already passed up the opportunity for prevention!

Unfortunately, we may meet that person who expresses himself physically, not verbally, and then strikes out with aggression, seemingly from nowhere. Until healthcare organizations start identifying the emergence of aggression before it becomes conflict, events like Michael McDermott's assault on his workplace in Wakefield, Massachusetts will continue to puzzle them. McDermott's employer was given signs; Mike Stanley, a team projects leader, said that McDermott recently had been coming in late and his performance wasn't as good as it could have been. Co-workers said he had become quiet, surly and quirky. These are all signs that can enable an individual to engage and prevent aggression in the first place. According to Denenberg and Braverman, violent behavior occurs due to three factors:

- A person who has poor coping mechanisms when stressed;
- The presence of increased stress in the workplace, which may be related to loss of employment or income; and
- A failure of the workplace to recognize the stress-related breakdown of the individual and to intercede prior to the violent episode.

This model supports the Aggression Continuum as described here, in that poorly managed stress is the major contributing factor to the escalation of an individual unable to cope with prevailing circumstances. Escalation to physical violence then occurs in an environment that promoted the behavior by not recognizing it earlier.

Healthcare and social service personnel are confronted face-to-face with individuals of both stable and unstable emotions and with a broad *spectrum* of problems and instabilities. One certified Aggression Management instructor and health provider, Deborah Leporowski, a doctor of psychology, is employed by the Veterans Administration in South Florida. Every day, five days a week, she interviews a continuing stream of veterans, most from the Vietnam era, whose touch with reality may be marginal. Deborah has spoken about a subculture of lost men who collect and carry firearms, often wear soiled and ragged camouflage, are unable to hold jobs, have abandoned or been abandoned by family and may have spent the past week sleeping in a wooded area behind a shopping center. She makes the point that these men, who number in uncounted thousands across the country, are the final victims of Vietnam, or any war, doomed perhaps to suffer a lifetime from what used to be called "battle fatigue" but is now clinically termed post-traumatic stress disorder (PTSD). The danger for Deborah and other veterans counselors is that they are not benign in their attitude about the course of their lives, but angry and bitter, and coiled so tightly that they may be *looking* for an excuse to explode.

The aggressor in healthcare is not always a patient, their family, a gang or gang member, or finally, a fellow employee. Sometimes the aggressor is a physician. On occasion nurses come in contact with physicians who are immensely talented in their medical abilities, but have little or no interpersonal skills. These physicians can become dictatorial, demanding and abusive. One account had an operating room physician grabbing the back of a nurse's head, shoving her face into the cavity of the patient's body and yelling "Can't you see that!" All too often hospital administration will do nothing about this behavior for fear of upsetting a lucrative financial stream, and as a result, most reports of violence by physicians are done anecdotally. When called into account for their actions, the interview is often conducted behind closed door among their peers, so that disciplinary action is often minimal, if taken at all.

If taught, nurses could utilize Aggression Management skills in their everyday practice, particularly in addressing aggression with physicians. They would learn techniques to decrease their own stress in order to respond more appropriately. Instead of choosing to avoid the confrontation, they would know first to reduce their own stress through cycle breathing techniques. Then, with a calm that would undermine the physician's aggression, they could respond verbally in an appropriate manner conveying a secure, self-confident presence, without threatening or inciting.

Chances are, when a doctor realizes a nurse is confident and unshaken by his actions he will back away from his aggression. Further escalation will place the physician at significant risk for a lawsuit and potentially other actions, which could include a suspension or termination of practice privileges. A calm, self-assured, non-threatening response strategy has been effective for nurses in the past; but remember, no two circumstances are the same, so individuals should always use their professional judgment.

Too often, healthcare organizations deny the existence of the many forms of non-physical aggression that are pervasive throughout their organization, i.e., verbal and emotional abuse, and bullying. Denial of aggressive/violent behavior results in the lack of a prevention program that allows for early recognition and management of the behavior. Possibly one of the most important elements to be included in an aggression/violence-in-the-workplace prevention program is the Aggression Continuum as noted in Figure 10.1. This graphic provides a mechanism to measure the escalation of aggression. It identifies where the aggressor and the Aggression Manager are on the Aggression Continuum, thereby providing the Aggression Manager with the opportunity to select the most effective skills to defuse anger in either the aggressor

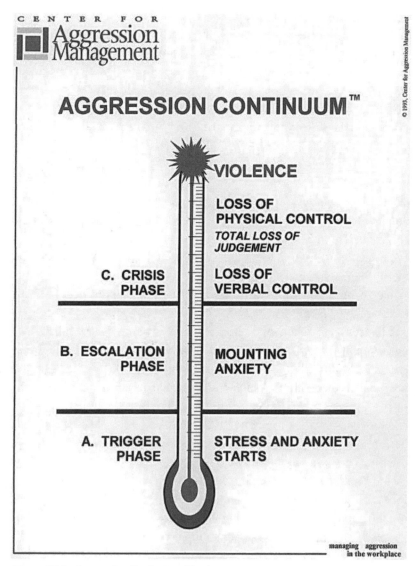

CENTER FOR
**Aggression
Management**

© 1993, Center for Aggression Management

AGGRESSION CONTINUUM™

VIOLENCE

LOSS OF
PHYSICAL CONTROL

*TOTAL LOSS OF
JUDGEMENT*

**C. CRISIS
PHASE**

LOSS OF
VERBAL CONTROL

**B. ESCALATION
PHASE**

**MOUNTING
ANXIETY**

**A. TRIGGER
PHASE**

**STRESS AND ANXIETY
STARTS**

managing aggression
in the workplace

Figure 10.1   *Aggression Continuum, Simple*

or themselves. It offers the opportunity to identify aggression before it becomes conflict so that aggression can be prevented rather than simply reacted to. Finally, the Aggression Continuum provides a template for the Aggression Manager to document the incident, maximizing his or her opportunity to illustrate the professional manner in which he or she dealt with the most difficult circumstances.

Some healthcare organizations are viewing this subject in the context of the total environment. Sometimes referred to as Enterprise Risk Management, this is when aggression and violence is viewed from the perspective of how it effects all other aspects of the healthcare business. This demonstrates the direct link between aggression in the healthcare environment and productivity. Even the Royal Mail has determined its cost from "employee friction" to be £247,000,000 per year. Do you know what the cost of aggression is in your healthcare workplace? When there are aggressors in your workforce, *no one else wants to be there*. Such a condition causes tardiness, absenteeism and ultimately turnover. The costs to productivity and the bottom line are profound. Diminished aggression in healthcare yields greater productivity. Imagine a future where productivity is significantly enhanced and employee satisfaction is at an all time high.

We have all heard about violence in healthcare, and with the National Institute for Occupational Safety and Health (NIOSH) declaring that more non-fatal assaults occur in healthcare than any other industry, we now must make every reasonable effort to protect doctors, nurses, other employees, patients and their families from this potential tragedy.

The message that the term "violence" conveys is misleading. It conjures up violent crimes and fatalities. Too often administrators who have not experienced a shooting in the past are likely to discount healthcare violence as an issue. When you consider solutions to healthcare violence, you tend to arrive at "crisis management." I have a crisis, I need to manage it. This is a reactive solution—*not* a preventive one. With the lives of healthcare employees and patients at risk, we must provide "prevention," not merely crisis management.

CHAPTER 11

Public Service . . . Public Violence—Part 1

"Going Postal" Is a Myth, but . . .

by Frank Readus

The cliché "going postal" has sprung from a contemporary American myth, an unintentional yet destructive media hoax that has been perpetrated on every employee of the U.S. Postal Service.

As you no doubt recall seeing on TV and in the press, the United States Postal Service was beset by a series of fatal shootings at various post offices in the late 1980s and 1990s.

Concerns about tensions and safety of postal employees in the workplace were frequently raised in the news media, sometimes to overblown proportions. Indeed, the news media did the "overkill" on coverage surrounding those fatal killings, and in doing so, violated the Postal Service employees' view of the security that they have in the workplace.

In 1998, in order to address employees' safety concerns, the United States Postal Service asked Joseph A. Califano, Jr., director of the National Center on Addiction and Substance Abuse at Columbia University, to lead a panel analyzing the issue. Joseph Califano and his panel concluded: "Going postal is a myth and a bad rap, causing unnecessary apprehension and fear among 900,000 postal workers." He also asserted that postal workers are only a third as likely as those in the national work force to become victims of homicide on the job.

Having put that myth to rest, however, the Califano report went on to testify that there was indeed a substantial problem of aggression throughout the U.S. Postal Service. As a result of this problem, postal employees still hold the belief that they are at greater risk than the average American worker of being a victim of workplace violence. They also perceive that "many managers and supervisors try to provoke employees to violence" and that postal employees generally have negative attitudes about managers and co-workers.

One obvious point the Califano report failed to focus on is the loss of productivity and other fiduciary damages that tend to trail workplace aggression. The Royal Mail, in the United Kingdom, claims that the cost of "employee friction" is 247,000,000 British pounds a year. There is a direct correlation between aggression in the workplace and productivity. When there are aggressors in the workplace, no one wants to be there. The result is tardiness, then absenteeism and finally turnover; all of which profoundly affect productivity. This aggression can easily be seen described within the Califano commission's report "Fears about Workplace Violence":

- Postal employees are six times likelier to believe they are at greater risk than the average worker to be a victim of workplace violence from co-workers. Less likely to agree that their employer "takes action to protect employees against violence by non-employees."
- More likely to say they fear being robbed or attacked at work.
- More likely to agree that "many managers and supervisors try to provoke employees to violence."
- Twice as likely as those in the national workforce to say they would accept a job offer from a different employer with the same wages, retirement and fringe benefits.
- Twice as likely as those in the national workforce to have negative attitudes about co-workers.
- Less likely than those in the national workforce to have positive attitudes about managers.

These are the reasons why aggression continues within the USPS and why productivity is not being maximized. There is thus a direct bearing between aggression in the workplace and productivity. As long as aggression in the USPS workplace is not addressed, employees will harbor an innate fear of going to work. This results in tardiness, absenteeism (often expressed as sick days) and even frequent employee turnover. All these events dampen productivity, cause plan failure and loss of revenue.

So, until concepts of aggression prevention are adopted, there will always be residual aggression within the United States Postal Service, maximum productivity will not be achieved, and committees will continue to study and recommend higher postage rates and curtailed delivery service in the pursuit of profitability.

The fact that the United States Postal Service is the second largest employer in the country, with close to 900,000 employees coming from very diverse origins and backgrounds, makes addressing the workplace aggression issue very complicated and sometimes very sensitive.

It's important to point out that the U.S. Postal Service is certainly not unique. The inherent pressures and stress of deadline-driven requirements, the diversity of personalities and cultural origins and the intensity of workplace politics are all problems that haunt many large corporations. Every point made, every problem highlighted, could apply to *your* organization as well.

So what solution should the Postal Service, or any organization, adopt to nip on the job aggression in the bud? Should one adopt conflict resolution and anger management as a means to an end? When conflict resolution is utilized, the opportunity to prevent aggression is already gone—and someone probably has been hurt. With anger management, there is no way to measure anger and thereby manage such intangible outrage. In the United States Postal Service, there is a level of tolerance for assertive behavior, which can be very positive and productive. When it comes to aggressive attitudes and behavior there is zero tolerance, because such behavior leads to physical confrontation and ultimately violence.

If all we intend to do is to react to aggression we will, eventually, be confronted with physical violence. If we have employees waiting for others to go "nose-to-nose" (conflict resolution) before they engage, eventually they will confront someone who does not communicate verbally, who will strike out physically; God forbid they have a weapon and they pull the trigger. Everyone says "where did that come from!" It came because no one was looking for aggression until it became conflict, and that was too late.

Even when it comes to negotiations between union and management, adopting a cooperative and constructive stance yields better results for both parties than displaying adversarial posturing and destructive belligerence.

Hence, the United States Postal Service adoption of Aggression Management skills is a very important approach toward identifying the possible emergence of aggression. Line employees and management can engage in a détente before conflict and physical violence rears its ugly head.

As previously indicated, the U.S. Postal Service is not unique. Regardless of the specific industry or corporation, a safe working environment is everyone's responsibility and concern, from hourly workers and white-collar employees to top management and the stockholders who expect return on their investment.

In applying Aggression Management skills in solving conflicts, both union and management have the opportunity to talk in an atmosphere of cooperative engagement, fostering amicable solutions to problems on the job. This approach has the potential to transform the United States Postal Service, or any organization, into a national model of a safe and secure workplace—the key to long-term productivity and profitability.

CHAPTER 12

Public Service . . . Public Violence—Part 2

Can Law Enforcement Prevent Crime?

written in consultation with Dave Bodie,
Bodie Consulting Services, Inc.

Law enforcement is a dangerous profession. Police chiefs and sheriffs pride themselves on ensuring that their officers are as well equipped as possible to handle the dangers of the job. They equip their officers with the newest semi-automatic firearms and the most effective impact weapons. They are always looking for "better" non-lethal force options. They devote considerable portions of their entry level and in-service training programs to teaching firearms training and use of force options. This training is important and it is necessary because it saves lives.

However, many of these same chiefs and sheriffs have neglected to adequately train their officers on the one weapon they will use more often than all others. They have failed to ensure that their officers have the verbal and interpersonal skills they need to not only effectively handle *aggressive* individuals, but to also control *their own* levels of aggression!

WHY AGGRESSION MANAGEMENT?

Law Enforcement in a Hostile Nation

Across America, public safety and security professionals are being asked to perform their duties in situations that are increasingly more confrontational and heated. "Road rage" and "air rage" are two new terms in the American lexicon that describe the national upsurge in anger. Everyday we see and hear reports of how our society is becoming less civil and less polite. In too many instances, this lack of civility escalates into anger and violence.

At the same time, almost paradoxically, society has increased its expectations of law enforcement officers. In an ever more hostile society, they are expected to be polite, even tempered and to use restraint in all of their encounters with the public. They are frequently accused, even by the most violent suspects, of being brutal and of using excessive force. Many officers remember the impact that the videotape of the Rodney King incident had on both law enforcement and the community.

According to Morris Womack and Finely Hayden in their book, *Communication: A Unique Significance for Law Enforcement*, "Police officers estimate they spend at least 75–90% of their time in some form of communication. But police training has not proportionately reflected this fact. It is estimated that less than 10% of training time is devoted to learning communications skills."

Roland Ouellette, in his book, *Management of Aggressive Behavior*, says, "Most human services personnel are not trained to use verbal skills, and agree that under stress they often shout commands out of frustration, not knowing how to handle the situation verbally."

Dave Bodie, one of my certified Aggression Management instructors, heads his own consulting firm in Maryland that trains police officers. Dave points out that managing aggression for law enforcement officers involves both carrying out a public duty to preserve the peace, detect crime and arrest violators, while at the same time maintaining the self-discipline required to be an effective Aggression Manager. These two responsibilities often run at cross-purposes, leading to frustration and anger on the part of police officers.

In *The Cutting Edge of Police Integrity*, Neal Trautman cites a study of police officers across the country that were decertified (had their police powers permanently removed) between 1990 and 1995. This research showed that almost 20% of these officers were decertified for anger-related offenses, i.e., excessive use of force, battery, weapons offenses and domestic offenses. Simply stated, they didn't have the skills they needed to manage their own aggression!

The same techniques I teach plant supervisors, human resource specialists and even office receptionists—controlling adrenaline to control the self—are even more critical to police officers who have to handle suspects who may be intoxicated, under the influence of drugs or even psychotic. An improperly managed incident, even a traffic ticket, can escalate from a verbal disagreement to the point where the police officer uses physical force.

Use of physical force presents a different threshold for each police officer. Nevertheless, commonalities emerge. Kenneth Adams, in an article entitled "What We Know about Police Use of Force," cites the following conclusions about this controversial topic:

- Police use force infrequently.
- Police use of force typically occurs at the lower end of the force spectrum, involving grabbing, pushing or shoving.
- Use of force typically occurs when police are trying to make an arrest and the suspect is resisting.
- Use of force appears to be unrelated to an officer's personal characteristics, such as age, gender or ethnicity.
- Use of force appears more likely to occur when police are dealing with persons under the influence of alcohol or drugs, or with mentally ill individuals, although more research is needed.
- A small proportion of officers seem to be disproportionately involved in use-of-force incidents.

Recently, law enforcement has been accused of practicing racial profiling, which is described as stopping minority group members for a traffic violation solely based upon their ethnicity. "Driving while black" is a hot topic. It has gathered national attention. President Bush, in his initial budget address to Congress, committed to having the Attorney General draft legislation to stop illegal racial profiling. It is driving the minority community and our law enforcement officers further and further apart. Many minority members no longer trust the police. And some officers are saying that they won't stop minority individuals who commit minor traffic violations because they don't want to be labeled as racist.

Yet, as the figures above indicate, some officers have been guilty of using excessive force. And, some members of the profession have been guilty of racial profiling. However, I believe that these incidents don't occur as frequently as the opponents of law enforcement would have you believe, but that they probably occur more often than the supporters of law enforcement are willing to admit.

A SOLUTION—COMMUNITY POLICING

For more than ten years, law enforcement has been slowly changing to a new style of policing, *community policing*. Many people are saying that this new style of policing is responsible for the substantial decreases in crime that has been occurring across the country. Community policing is based on the police, local government and the community working together to identify and resolve crime problems. Departments have devoted considerable resources to developing the strong police/community partnerships that are needed to make community policing work. In many of our inner cities, police/community relations are stronger than ever.

Poor Public Image

However, one poorly handled incident can undo all of these efforts. Dr. George Thompson and Jerry Jenkins reported in their book, *Verbal Judo—The Gentle Art of Persuasion*, that "research shows that if someone has a bad experience with a police officer he will tell 27 to 28 people over the next three days." The great majority of these encounters don't involve brutality. Surprisingly, they don't even involve the use of force. They happen when citizens feel that they were treated and spoken to in a disrespectful manner.

A Reputation for Using Excessive Force

An improperly managed incident can escalate from a verbal disagreement to the point where the officer uses physical force. In most instances, after a detailed internal investigation, the officer is found to have acted within his department's use-of-force guidelines. Although this resolution may make the officer feel better, it can also lead to a perception by the community that the police are covering up and are protecting their own. (Remember the "us" and "them" syndrome.)

If you were to ask the accused officer, "if you could have handled the incident differently, and still achieved your objective, would you have done so?" Most officers would reply "absolutely!" These officers want to do a professional job! They want to be better equipped to handle these situations. However, they realize that they are missing the tools they need to effectively handle people under stressful situations. Aggression Management can give them the verbal and interpersonal tools they need to effectively handle these situations.

Too Many Injured Officers

A police officer knows that physical force is the last thing the officer wants. Dave Bodie points out some advice he got years ago as a rookie cop from a veteran on the force, "Dave, the best thing that can happen to you in a fight is that you come out the same way you went in." He was telling Dave that given enough fights, he would eventually sustain a major injury. That translates to a mandate to minimize physical confrontations. How? By using Aggression Management to dissuade a suspect from using force or violence.

An improperly handled street encounter can quickly change from a verbal encounter to one that results in the use of physical force. In extreme cases, it can even escalate to the point where deadly force is used. According to National Crime Victimization Survey, the law enforcement profession has the highest rate of workplace violence, more than convenience/liquor stores, gas stations, bars and other retail businesses combined. In many departments, almost as many officers receive disability retirement as normal retirement. We need to do a better job of providing our officers with a safer workplace. We need to do as much as we can to reverse this trend.

High Personnel Turnover Rate

If a department has a poor public image, or a reputation for using excessive force, or a high rate of work-related injuries, it is not a good place to work. Eventually, if these problems are not corrected, that department will find that its best and most experienced officers are either leaving for other law enforcement agencies or are leaving the profession completely. Law enforcement, and indeed our society, cannot afford to lose its best and brightest police officers, because such a loss dangerously reduces the level of protection and security we enjoy and all too often take for granted.

USING AGGRESSION MANAGEMENT IN LAW ENFORCEMENT

Can law enforcement actually prevent crime? Sheriff Don Eslinger of Seminole County, Florida, believes it can, but only with the cooperation of the community. Sheriff Eslinger has hired the Center for Aggression Management to teach selected deputies Aggression Management skills. These deputies will then be available to the Seminole County community to teach individuals the skills to identify the emergence of aggression and foresee the possibility of conflict. This will enables them to engage and prevent aggression before it becomes an incident or a violent crime. The deputies will be able to teach these valuable skills, free of charge, to community homeowner associations, businesses, civic organizations and churches.

Others in the law enforcement community are waiting for individuals to express their aggression *in conflict or a violent crime* before they take any action. The only skills being offered today are conflict resolution skills, which presuppose conflict, and deny law enforcement officers any opportunity to prevent aggression. Eventually they will meet that person who expresses himself physically, not verbally, and then strikes out with aggression that seems to come from nowhere.

Until we, both as a community and as individuals, start identifying the emergence of aggression before it becomes conflict, events like Michael McDermott's assault on his workplace in Wakefield, Massachusetts will continue to puzzle us. However, we shouldn't be puzzled! There were warning signs that should have been heeded. Mike Stanley, a team projects leader, said that McDermott recently had been coming in late and his performance wasn't as good as it could have been. Co-workers referred to him as quiet, surly and quirky. These are all signs that enable an individual to engage and prevent aggression in the first place.

The Future of Aggression Management and Law Enforcement

Okay, let's suppose that Aggression Management is accepted by the law enforcement profession. How will its acceptance change law enforcement? What effects will it have on how law enforcement officers deliver services to their communities? What effects will its acceptance and use have on our society?

The Arts of Aggression Management and the Use of Force Continuum

Society has given law enforcement officers the responsibility for arresting individuals who are either committing crimes or are endangering public safety. And, to fulfill this responsibility, society has also given them the authority to use reasonable force to make an arrest.

However, society also expects law enforcement officers to exercise their authority properly. To ensure that physical force is used in a legal and reasonable manner, law enforcement agencies have developed strict guidelines that carefully delineate when, and to what degree, force is authorized. These guidelines vary from agency to agency and are referred to as the "Use of Force Continuum."

Most confrontations between law enforcement and individuals start with an encounter that can be resolved by using effective interpersonal and communications skills. The same skills that are included in the Arts of Aggression Management. Dave and I believe that in the future, law enforcement agencies will include the skills of Aggression Management and the Aggression Continuum as a more complete tool to identify the emergence of aggression, to foresee the possibility of conflict, and to enable the officer to engage and prevent conflict.

How Will These Skills Be Taught?

New officers will be taught these skills when they attend the police academy. Veteran officers will learn them during in-service training.

RESISTANCE LEVELS	1. Presence	1. Interview Stance	2. Verbal Direction	2. Dialoque	2. Touch	3. Restraint Devices	3. Transporters	3. Take Downs	3. Pain Compliance	3. Counter Moves	4. Intermediate Weapons	5. Incapacitation	6. Deadly Force
6. Aggravated Physical	✓	✓	✓	✓	✓	✓	✓	✓	✓	✓	✓	✓	✓
5. Aggressive Physical	✓	✓	✓	✓	✓	✓	✓	✓	✓	✓	✓	✓	
4. Active Physical	✓	✓	✓	✓	✓	✓	✓	✓	✓	✓	✓		
3. Passive Physical	✓	✓	✓	✓	✓	✓	✓	✓	✓				
2. Verbal	✓	✓	✓	✓	✓	✓							
1. Presence	✓	✓	✓	✓	✓								

RESPONSE LEVELS

Figure 12.1   Use of Force Matrix (Adapted from Florida Department of Law Enforcement, 1994.)

They will be taught as a vital component of the more complete use-of-force training.

They will not however, be taught as a separate block of instruction. Instead, they will be taught as part of a process for dealing with people under stressful situations. For example, officers will first learn the basic skills and techniques of Aggression Management in a classroom setting.

Later, we envision that officers will participate in a realistic, high-stress training scenario involving thoroughly briefed role players. For example, one scenario may be a simulated traffic stop involving real vehicles and a trainer who role-plays as the violator. The violator may become verbally aggressive. The officer will be expected to recognize the signs of rising aggression and use the appropriate strategies to diffuse the aggressor. After the scenario, which has been videotaped, the student and the trainers will critique the student's performance.

In another scenario, the student officers may have to respond to a family fight between a husband and wife. Again, the students will have to be able to recognize the signs of rising aggression and attempt to diffuse it. Trainers know that the more realistic the training is, the greater the level of comprehension and retention. This type of training will ensure that when needed, officers will be able to use the Arts of Aggression Management to reduce aggression and to increase the safety of victims, violators and themselves. In this way, officers will be better enabled to prevent aggression and violent crime in their communities.

The Center for Aggression Management and Law Enforcement Training

The Center for Aggression Management is working with Bodie Consulting Services, Inc. to ensure that it offers the law enforcement community the best training possible.

We are committed to continuously improving our course content and training methods to ensure that they meet the needs of our ever-changing society. These improvements will keep the center on the cutting-edge of Aggression Management training, while helping law enforcement agencies to better prevent violent crime in their community.

CHAPTER 13

Managing Aggression in the Retail Food Service Industry
by Scott Vasatka, Human Asset Management, Inc.

Virginia, July 1997, 5:00 p.m.
A car pulled up to a fast-food drive-through window and the driver made an insulting comment to the cashier. The cashier responded with name calling. The customer threw his drink back through the window, splashing it everywhere. All the restaurant employees stormed out into the parking lot and blocked the car preventing it from leaving, all the while taunting the driver. The driver revved his engine as if about to run down the employees. Fortunately, the police arrived before anyone was hurt. It was a neighbor, not the manager, who called the police. Later, the manager admitted she felt helpless trying to stop the employees, because they had reached a point beyond her control.

North Carolina, May 1999, 6:00 p.m.
A female customer pulled up to the drive-through window. The female cashier had had a previous run-in with this customer off-duty over a boyfriend. They began to argue, trade insults and even throw food. Finally, the enraged customer put her car in park, and actually crawled through the drive-through window to attack the restaurant employee. A furious fight lasted for several minutes after the customer was in the restaurant. Later, the manager admitted not knowing what to do when this situation started to escalate.

Tennessee, December, 1999, 7:00 a.m.
An hourly employee became increasingly upset with his manager over what his duties were to be that day. After loud and escalating arguments, the employee murdered his manager, then sought out the only

other employee on duty, who was working in the walk-in cooler, and murdered her. This employee lived in the area and had gone to high school with several of the other employees. He later confessed to police that he was "having a bad day," and that the manager had yelled at him during their argument, which upset him to the point of beating her to death. He then decided to murder the other employee and stage it as an attempted robbery.

Illinois, April 2000, 11:00 p.m.
The manager was closing the restaurant with several employees when a robber entered the restaurant though the back door. The manager was forced to open the safe and the other crewmembers were made to lie down on the floor. After the safe was emptied the manager was also forced to the floor, and the robber fled the building. The manager admitted later that he felt violated. The robber had called them names and had been exceptionally cruel in his treatment of them. The manager had been working very hard to turn around a failing restaurant, and took all this abuse of his people personally. He got up from the floor, told an employee to call the police, and ran after the robber. He caught him—only to be beaten nearly to death by the robber. The restaurant lost $3,000 to the robber, and also paid $62,000 in workers compensation claims.

Food service is one of the most basic segments of the retail market, since it provides one of our most fundamental needs—food. The restaurant industry serves the entire spectrum of customers, budgets and dining preferences—from fast food restaurants to the breakfast-lunch-dinner cafes, to casual, "family-priced" restaurants that usually offer alcohol, to upscale gourmet restaurants that make dining out a social event, and food preparation an art form.

The restaurant industry employs 11 million people, making it the largest employer outside the government. In 1999, according to the National Restaurant Association, almost half of all adults, 44%, were restaurant patrons during a typical day. With these statistics, it's easy to see how much the food service industry has become a part of all of our lives. The other indisputable evidence are the ubiquitous "Help

Wanted" signs, which seem to be permanent fixtures in so many restaurant windows.

This combination of increasing sales and the constant need for replacement personnel is the recipe for more and more aggression in the food service industry. Violence by both customers and employees underscores the need to manage aggression in food service. The emergence of aggression in the food service industry is due to several factors inherent in the business: the frantic "turn and burn" pace of the fast food environment; the element of alcohol in family and fine dining establishments; and the predominance of younger, less educated employees with limited loyalties and high turnover.

To quote from the Occupational Safety and Health Administration (OSHA) arm of the U.S. Department of Labor, *nearly 1,000 workers are murdered and 1.5 million are assaulted in the workplace each year.*

Environmental conditions associated with workplace assaults have been identified and control strategies have been implemented in a number of work settings. OSHA has developed guidelines and recommendations to reduce worker exposure to violence, but has not yet issued any rules. However, OSHA knows that, although their guidelines are voluntary, attorneys and the courts will use these guidelines as standards to impose civil liability against food service employers.

AN HR PROFESSIONAL'S PERSPECTIVE

As a Human Resources and Risk Management Executive of a major fast food chain of over 380 locations, I have investigated wide-ranging incidents of workplace violence. These include a customer crawling through a drive-through window to attack one of our employees; and one of our employees brutally murdering his manager and another employee because, "She yelled at me." It is important to note that in this particular incident there were no previous acts or record of violence by this individual at this place of employment or in his past employment history.

Stories such as these are becoming far too commonplace in the food service industry. If all we intend to do is to react to such aggression we will, eventually, be confronted with physical violence. But if our responsibility is the safety of those in our organization, we need to *prevent* such violence as opposed to waiting until we have to react to it. As incidents of aggression escalate, it has become more and more apparent that current methods for preventing aggression and violence in our restaurants are not working.

As we look at conventional means of managing aggression, we see topics like conflict resolution and anger management, which are fatally flawed. Conflict resolution presupposes conflict; you are already reacting; you are already passed beyond any opportunity to prevent aggression. If we only train our employees to respond when two individuals are in "nose-to-nose" conflict, eventually someone who communicates physically rather than verbally will strike out violently "out of nowhere." God forbid they have a weapon.

If we are to achieve prevention, we must adhere to an accepted business axiom: if you can measure it, you can manage it. The problem with anger management is that we all measure anger differently and therefore experience and express it differently. There has been no common denominator or yardstick with which we could measure anger.

But now, the Center for Aggression Management has developed the Aggression Continuum, a means by which to measure aggression in others and in ourselves. This easily applied scale can empower our employees with the skills to identify the emergence of aggression before it becomes conflict, so that they can engage and prevent aggression, not merely react to it.

Do you have any idea what the cost of aggression is in your restaurant or restaurant chain? That cost is greater than you think. When there are aggressors in your workforce, for example, no one else wants to be there. This causes tardiness, absenteeism and finally turnover. The cost to productivity is profound. As has been pointed out previously, the United Kingdom's Royal Mail has determined that the cost from "employee friction," or aggression, is approximately £247,000,000 per year.

I am convinced that training in Aggression Management must become part of our basic management training programs. Such training is crucial because we as employers have a moral and, according to OSHA, a statutory obligation to train our employees to react to any known dangers we feel exist in the workplace. It is also necessary as a well-grounded strategy of boosting sales, reducing turnover and improving the overall quality of life our employees enjoy at the workplace.

TRAINING

The ASTD, American Society for Training and Development, based in Alexandria, Virginia, outlined the following in its 2001 State of the Industry Report.

1. While the average company is training record levels of employees—78.6 percent—Mark Van Buren, Director of Research for ASTD, said, "It's important to note that the top 10 percent of companies surveyed train 98.4 percent of employees in their organizations."
2. The top 10 percent of companies surveyed, or "Training Investment Leaders" also spent an average of $1,665 on training per eligible employee, compared to $677 for the average survey respondent. Training Investment Leaders have made learning a central focus of organization-wide efforts to stay competitive and deliver results in the New Economy.
3. The study's key findings also indicate a few surprises, according to Van Buren. "The training landscape is shifting, in part because of the rapid rate of change many firms have been experiencing," he said. "Training, like any other financial investment, is not immune to changing times. Now, more than ever, companies must continually demonstrate the value and worth of their investments in training."
4. The largest share of spending on training went to training in technical processes and procedures (13 percent), with professional skills following close behind (11 percent). *Interpersonal communication*, new employee orientation, and IT skills followed at 9 percent each.

As ASTD points out, more and more we are seeing a shift in our industry to training in areas of *interpersonal skill sets,* and we are noticing increasing awareness of the fact that *how people work effectively with each other* is as important as their technical training.

Human relations training programs such as Aggression Management are one overlying skill development area that can have a positive impact in virtually every aspect of our business. Such training is already proving effective in substantially reducing workplace violence, and lessening the need for costly conflict resolution, which today often takes on the form of a legal claim in either the EEOC, Department of Human Rights, or a court of law.

OUR LEGAL OBLIGATIONS TO TRAIN AND COMMUNICATE

In today's litigious society, all too often we are pulled into the legal arena, not only for what we may have done, but also in many cases for what we have failed to do, or in other words, negligence.

As the workplace violence in the country continues to escalate, so also, in the eyes of the law and our legal community, does our obligation as employers to inform and train our employees in order to prevent to the fullest extent possible any potential aggression.

This failure to provide a safe working environment for employees stems from, in my experience, two sources. The first is negligent hiring. We fail to take prudent steps to insure that we don't hire people who are either a high risk in our environment, or have misrepresented themselves in a manner that reference or background checks should have revealed.

We hesitate to act decisively and immediately when employees of ours have displayed, through words or actions, that they may have become a threat to their co-workers or our customers. We, as restaurateurs, are equally as liable whether we knowingly or unknowingly leave our workplace harmful to our employees. Regardless, the courts will deem that we should have known.

Much as we install fire suppression systems and sprinklers as well as a fire evacuation procedure and plan for the safety of employees and customers, we must also manage the aggression in our establishments, as well as teach our staff the Art of Safe Escape. The key to prevention of aggression in the workplace is to train our employees to recognize its emergence in co-workers, customers and themselves, foresee the possibility of conflict and offer the skills to prevent aggression before it becomes conflict. Of course, if aggression has escalated, employees must know how to manage it to safe levels, or remove themselves as a target utilizing proactive safe escape plans as outlined in Aggression Management methodologies. Working with the Center for Aggression Management, we have developed a comprehensive system of Aggression Management training for our food service clients that can be easily incorporated into their restaurant training systems for staff and management. The result will be a safer workplace for employees and customers, significantly reduced hiring and training costs, and the lessening of exposure to expensive litigation. Any one of these benefits makes Aggression Management training a value well worth our time and expense.

CHAPTER 14

Can a Terrorist Be Identified Before He Takes His Seat?

Since the tragic events of September 11, 2001, our approach to vigilance has profoundly changed. As I write it is important to note that, although I am not an expert on terrorism, per se. My contribution comes as an expert in Aggression Management.

We at the Center for Aggression Management have been teaching individuals proven skills to identify and measure the emergence of aggression prior to conflict thereby empowering us to prevent aggression. This ability to identify and measure aggression is what we can offer to this cause.

We know that through these skills, along with an effective interview process, we can identify a potential terrorist. We have heard many references to *technical intelligence* versus *human intelligence*. Albeit technical intelligence is vital, there is a clear and present need for greater and more effective human intelligence.

THE ISSUE

Airline personnel struggle with the volume of passengers and how to effectively select individuals for thorough evaluation. Most airlines are using some form of profiling, whether El Al's (a five category profiling system) or APS (Advanced Passenger Screening, used by United on September 11, 2001, at Boston's Logan International Airport) or CAPS (Computer-Assisted Passenger Screening) or RAPS (defined simply as: "a set of sophisticated procedures which seek to identify a potential threat, before it materializes, through a methodology of risk evaluation and classification of passengers") each is flawed by the very nature of profiling.

To illustrate why profiling is flawed, we use the U.S. Secret Service's report on Targeted Violence in Schools. Although this is directed to students, we believe it also applies to adults. "The use of profiles is not effective either for identifying students who may pose a risk for targeted violence at school or—once a student has been identified—for assessing the risk that a particular student may pose for school-based targeted violence." It continues, "An inquiry should focus instead on a student's behaviors and communications to determine if the student appears to be planning or preparing for an attack."

These are the measures we use. We use behavior, body language and communication indicators to measure an aggressor's escalation. While others do use behavior and body language to some degree, we have developed a proven method of measuring these elements, making it easier for an interviewer to measure the ticket-holder or "selectee's" indicators for terrorism. The important question becomes, "Do I allow this person on that plane?" If you cannot measure aggression, you cannot answer that question! This is why our method of measuring aggression becomes an essential tool.

Profile screening can be an important tool. Interview screening is an essential tool. It is our opinion that identifying and measuring a terrorist's aggression prior to him taking his seat on an airplane can be the final piece to prevent this kind of violence in our skies.

SIGNS OF A TERRORIST

Although there is no finite rule that applies to all humans, there are reliable cues that we can use to identify an emerging aggressor. It is not instinctual for one human to attack another human, therefore emerging aggressors must disconnect from their victims. We have heard that terrorists "find a calm" before they effect their attack. This occurs when individuals completely disconnect from their victim(s) and their own well-being. This typically causes the aggressor to exhibit certain behavior, body language and verbal communication that can be identified and measured. The center has developed a means to measure the emergence of both Primal Aggression and Cognitive Aggression. Combined with an effective interview process, these Primal and Cognitive Aggression Continuums can be a successful tool to detecting a potential terrorist. The current profiling systems (CAPS, APS, RAPS) leave a critical gap in our homeland security and the safety of United States citizens. The collective methods of measuring aggression and effective interviewing augment our current system and close this critical gap.

Table 14.1. Opportunities for Interviews

Checkpoints	NON-VERBAL AGGRESSION			VERBAL AGGRESSION	DESCRIPTION
	BEHAVIOR COGNITIVE	BEHAVIOR PRIMAL	BODY LANGUAGE		
At the check-in counter					
o Roaming assistant for those in line for ticketing and check-in (these screeners will begin observing potential passengers and their associates as they enter the terminal area)					
o At the check-in counter by the ticketing agent					
At the carry-on baggage inspection point					
o As the passengers' ticket is matched with their picture ID					
o As the passenger passes through the metal detector					
o Additional opportunity as the passenger is checked for carry-on items that are forbidden, dangerous and/or explosives					
At the terminal-side check-in point					
o As passengers check for seat assignments					
o As passengers ask for standby					
o Boarding agent as passengers enter the corridor to the plane					
Upon boarding the plane by the attendant					

Richard Reid exemplifies this need. Screeners in Paris intuitively knew there was a problem with Mr. Reid. The first day they prevented him from entering the aircraft but the second day they permitted him on board. This was possible only because the screeners were unable to measure aggression.

We suggest three levels of training: 1) basic screeners, 2) screener supervisors and 3) agency personnel (law enforcement certified). If we provide these skills only to law enforcement personnel, we miss an important opportunity to identify a potential terrorist.

Interviews: The Fear of Being Revealed and Their Mission Being Lost

Terrorists may not exhibit any emotion about their victims or themselves, but they are fearful that they will fail. Typically terrorists will illustrate specific body language, behavior and communication indicators when their mission is confronted in the interview process the center has developed a means to identify and measure these indicators.

Chapter 15

Aggression's Effect on Productivity

What's the Cost?

by Dr. Charles W. Coker

In today's corporate world, most people consider themselves professionals. They've graduated from high school, college, a trade school or have received months of training in their area of expertise. They feel competent in their ability to do their job. If you asked one of those individuals what they would ask of their management, they would probably respond, "Tell me what you want me to do, when you want it done, any irregularity from the norm and let me do it." Most people take pride in their work and want to be acknowledged for their efforts. The majority of employees do not want someone in his or her face being pushy, negative or aggressive. This type of behavior destroys focus and keeps the employee's mind on everything but their personal productivity. Aggression, especially, has a direct effect on an employee's performance and thereby the company's productivity and profitability.

Workplace aggression is like an invisible tornado, elevating stress, uncertainty and a loss of professionalism, until it explodes. It weaves in and out of the workforce creating havoc and damage as this "carrier" moves through the workplace. Employees who are touched by aggression feel disheveled, disoriented, wonder what hit them and are concerned that they may be blindsided again at any time. They become gun-shy very quickly, if not immediately. The result is that an employee has a lack of ability to concentrate, an elevation of fear, diminished personal motivation and possesses an inability to perform at normal expectation levels. Tragically, there is also a loss of pride in their work. The desire for personal achievement and recognition is lost to fear and worry as their security is questioned.

When there are aggressors in a workforce, no one else wants to be there. No one that I have met wants to be subjected to harassment, danger or even death. Most people would work for less and someplace else, even if it meant settling for less, rather than subject themselves to this type of work environment. Most employees under this type of stress respond with tardiness, absenteeism, turnover, and at minimum a less productive workday. Each of these factors cost companies big dollars. In the past organizations have either ignored, discounted or avoided the reality of the bottom line impact of aggression. This is no longer the case. Companies are now measuring the impact aggression has made on tardiness, absenteeism, turnover and all levels of productivity through accounting and management processes.

What are the effects of aggression on productivity? The United Kingdom's Royal Mail has determined that the cost from "employee friction" (i.e., aggression) is £247,000,000 per year or the equivalent of U.S. $400,000,000. The majority of companies in America with 50-plus employees are losing money due to aggression in the workplace; however, few are willing to admit it. These are the same companies that don't understand why their profitability is suffering. Some corporate leaders refuse to face the fact that they have hired dysfunctional, aggressive or even violent employees who are draining their profits as quickly as if a truck was backed up to their warehouse door, loaded up with their product and left without paying. There is a shortage of leaders educated with the skills necessary to recognize, manage and predict aggression in the workplace.

DO YOU KNOW WHAT THE COST OF AGGRESSION IS IN YOUR WORKPLACE?

Earlier we defined aggression as: *a forceful action or procedure, hostile, injurious, destructive behavior or outlook.* Since, aggression is no longer a mystery and has been refined to a science, company managers and supervisory leadership must be trained and educated in the necessary recognition of all aspects of the subject. If management is not educated there will not be progress in reducing and/or eliminating aggression from the workforce. If it is not minimized in the employee base, productivity will never be maximized and the stockholders will never receive their best *Return on Investment* (ROI). If profitability and/or peak performance are issues for your organization you will need to address aggression with a passion. Once that decision is made you can 1) learn to recognize the problem, 2) count the cost, and 3) develop a plan to diminish aggression and increase productivity.

Psychiatrists, psychologists and other behavioral experts have identified a myriad of causes for aggression and its corresponding violence. However, there is no aggressive behavior unless there are first aggressive thoughts. These thoughts are generated from belief systems that support a rationale for aggressive reaction to stimuli. One of the greatest innovations of recent history is the ability to identify and measure a *propensity* for aggression as it pertains to behavior, attitudes and personal motivation. Once these factors have been identified an effort can be made to change the human perspective and thereby positively impact aggressive reaction and behavior. This could range from identification of workplace policies that create an aggressive state to isolation of individuals who have aggressive tendencies.

STEP ONE: IDENTIFY

There are numerous methods of learning to recognize aggression. We will discuss the three most common, widely accepted and validated as well as successfully applied. Each has its own distinct advantages based on time and investment.

The first, most widely accepted and least expensive approach is by training employees to identify aggression, its signals and its phases from a general perspective. There are many common and easily identifiable traits that the average aggressor displays. These aggression "skills" can be categorized, catalogued and committed to memory. Employers can train employees, supervisors and managers to recognize the behavior associated with aggression in the same way they can recognize a defective part or software that is not functioning properly. Workers can then be rehearsed in how to meet and deal with each of these signals and phases leading to impending danger. The aggressive employee can be helped with his problem and in most circumstances quickly mainstreamed back into the workforce with appropriate direction and help.

The second approach is to expand on a solid foundation of Aggression Management skills. Most trained experts agree that every visible behavior is caused by underlying attitudes, values and motivations. Based on an individual's natural behavioral style his or her aggression will be foreshadowed and demonstrated differently. For example an extrovert will normally be more verbally aggressive, while an introvert will tend to be more passively aggressive. Both are potentially dangerous—one no more than the other. By developing in-depth understanding of behavior (using any of the behavioral models), attitudes and values as well as motivations, the Aggression Manager will be able to better predict the aggression that is most common to each behavioral style, attitude and value type, as well as motivations that are consistent with aggressive behavior. The manager will not be able to predict an aggressive event, but will be able to understand an employee's propensity toward specific types of aggression. There is great added value to this training with minimal costs associated with specialized training. Employees can be managed and evaluated much more quickly and with greater insight as to their propensity for a specific type of aggression.

Motivational assessment is a third and highly refined approach to identifying aggressive personalities in the workplace. This methodology is growing, after the publication of studies by R. Chris Martin, Ph.D. (UMKC), and others in identification of motivations consistent with the aggressive and violent mindset. This approach is not recommended as a substitute for Aggression Management training, as all employees need to be able to recognize the basics of aggressive behavior. Motivational assessment will provide appropriate information to the manager concerning the counter productive motivations that may cause an employee to become aggressive or violent. Motivational assessment will provide additional insight, not visible under other assessments, into an individual's propensity toward a type of aggression; it will not predict a specific incident. This information will help a manager identify how aggression will manifest itself, what it will probably look like and how long it will take to help the individual work through the challenges that are the foundation of his aggression. Assessment can also be a helpful tool in directing an employee to the right EAP program, if necessary. Additional costs will be incurred with this approach, as an employee must be certified in the administration and interpretation of this tool and its scoring. However, there has not been a case to this author's knowledge where the investment has not returned more than its costs.

STEP 2: COUNT THE COST

Aggression in the workplace has become an increasing problem for America and the rest of the world. Today, many organizations throughout the world continue to be blindsided by aggression in the workplace. The multinational organizations are no longer by themselves as evidenced by the carnage of a small hi-tech firm in Massachusetts, during Christmas 2000. Many large organizations have begun to investigate this phenomenon. They have recognized that prevention is necessary if the workforce is to become "safe" for the present and the future. An unsafe work environment does and will continue to negatively affect productivity and turnover, as well as its profitability. This translates into real dollars and can make the difference between a company that shows a profit and one that does not.

In the past aggression has been perceived as a cancer that grows silently undercover with what the general workforce sees as no outwardly visible signs. With the advent of our growing knowledge of aggression, there has also been a growth in the development of measuring the cost of aggression in the workplace. Accidents, absenteeism, turnover and low morale can all be attributed, in part, to aggression issues. Additionally, anxiety due to aggression can become paralyzing to the workforce. It is therefore important for upper management to recognize that there is a cost associated with aggression, and a financial benefit to providing effective prevention strategies on an ongoing basis. Since we now know, without doubt, that a firm's size is not an indicator of the potential for any or all acts of aggression; all companies must consider using the self-discovery process to count their own costs. One of the best approaches to eliminating the cost of aggression is to understand how deeply those costs cut into your own company's profits.

Aggression costs can be identified and measured within virtually any organization through relatively simple survey techniques. Most companies have internal procedures that monitor tardiness, absenteeism, turnover and levels of productivity through their present accounting and management processes. By supplementing your accepted procedures with the appropriate surveys the impact of aggression can be measured within your own organization. Surveys are available for line workers, supervisors and managers, as well as executive staff. These can be administered before or immediately after Aggression Management training. Recent studies conducted indicate that the most accurate findings and cost analysis are a result of post-training surveys, due to a better understanding of what aggression "looks like" in the workplace.

Numerous investigations, in multiple American industries, have been conducted over a period of several years to measure the cost of aggression on a company's bottom line. Initial findings of lost time wages, damage to equipment and premises, as well as legal costs are staggering when management conducts an honest and objective survey. Those studies have now been published and are available through the Center for Aggression Management. The studies empirically validate the ignored costs that have played havoc on corporate productivity in the past few decades.

Surveys can now be highly refined and customized to specific industries and varying work environments. The process, however, is standardized in all industries. The strategic process begins with a survey that reports specific aggression issues within an employer's organization. This information is then compiled and analyzed after the employees participate in Aggression Management training. All participants are anonymously given a twenty-one-item questionnaire consisting of both multiple choice and essay questions. All items are related directly to their perception of aggression, its impact on themselves, other individuals and the company as well as the Aggression Management skills and issues introduced during the training. The participants should be made up of managers, supervisors and other appropriate personnel, who represent all working groups. Male, female and minorities should be represented. All participants' primary language should be the same as the survey language. Respondents must represent all job descriptions, to insure the scope of aggression is measured properly. All participant responses are voluntary and anonymous, to ensure truthful responses.

Employee respondents, in every survey conducted by this author, believe that workplace aggression was a deep-seeded problem within every organization surveyed. The following data was extracted from two companies this author surveyed. Both companies had similar findings and closely associated loss costs.

- A staggering 92% of respondents indicated that they had been exposed to workplace aggression and it had an impact on their productivity.
- 85% of employees believe that the company can and should take steps to prevent workplace aggression.
- 76% of the participants believe that management is and should be held responsible for workplace aggression, if prevention training is not instituted. (These findings are consistent with the Califano Report conducted in August 2000, which stated "Employees are more likely to agree that many managers and supervisors try to provoke employees to violence. And this organization's employees are less likely to agree that their employer takes action to protect employees against violence by non-employees.")
- 100% of the survey participants indicated that skills training could diffuse or allow them to escape the danger associated with aggression.
- 67% of all surveyed employees had personal knowledge of aggression incidents that impacted productivity and cost the company money.
- 77% of the employee respondents verify that the company is losing money through damaged or destroyed property as a result of the stress-induced environment.
- Participants' estimates of costs involved are staggering, based on the type of incident that occurred. Estimates ranged from a low of $3,750 to some publicized incidents that cost $3,000,000 and one reported $50,000,000 settlement.

From these studies, this author has been able to determine the most common forms of manifested aggression as defined by the participant base. In their opinion, "aggression" embodies everything from verbal abuse through violent behavior. The employees specified:

- Sexual Harassment
- Bullying
- Management-Labor Conflict
- Domestic Violence Spillover
- Road Rage
- Student-Teacher Conflict
- Robbery
- Militancy-Terrorism
- Homicide

STEP 3: DEVELOP A PLAN FOR SUCCESS

Years of research, as well as the referred studies and multiple research projects conducted by this author and his staff conclude that the best plan for success is a preventive approach to aggression and violent behavior through a foundational knowledge of:

- Aggression is the core of everything from verbal abuse to violent behavior.
- Recognition of aggressive behavior enhanced by the ability to predict the type of aggression most common to the individual and their behavior.
- How to communicate with or persuade an aggressor.
- How to safely escape bodily injury and/or a potentially life threatening environment.

An additional benefit of the cited studies was the positive employee response to conceptual approaches for the elimination of aggression in the workplace. The participants were eager to be involved in the developmental process for the elimination of aggression in the workplace. Their feedback and enthusiastic participation provided the organization with an indication that the employee base sees an opportunity to diminish aggression, increase productivity and enhance their image as employees among themselves and to the public through this four-point training.

Participant feedback indicates that current employee and newly-hired employees' education in this arena would send a clear signal to everyone familiar with past documented incidents. Most importantly, it would provide a "starting point" for a process that would have a significant impact on a problem that is not just perceived but is real in their minds. Further it would provide an opportunity for morale improvement, which would trigger improved productivity. The respondents are not going to be happy until a "zero tolerance" policy actually exists. Only then will they feel safe. Critical to success is a systematic approach to employee accountability for diminished workplace aggression. This four-point approach would help diminish the staggering management responsibility once the superiors deliver planning, training and intervention sessions. Management would no longer have to carry the load of responsibility alone—the rank and file worker would own the process too!

It is this author's opinion that the knowledge of this training would continue to spread as each facility communicates with others, and refines the process most effective in the culture of the training organization. The company studied could take this opportunity and use it to their advantage to build momentum and capitalize on its publicity as well as public relations within the ranks of its employees.

Employers, regardless of their size must begin to take inventory of the cost of aggression in their workplace. Dedicated Aggression Management training can diminish aggression in the workplace. Aggression Management training, as it has been documented, can save lives, yield greater productivity and improves morale at a rate of $10 to $1 when compared to the cost of investment in technology (Suiter and Bonnstetter, "Individual Coping Strategies and Behavioral Style"). Australia has taken the lead by requiring 4% of a company's revenues to be dedicated to training. It is only when we invest in people that we get our best ROI. Imagine a future where productivity is significantly enhanced and employee safety and satisfaction are at an all time high because of a small investment in your employees.

CHAPTER 16

Becoming Part of the Solution

The urgent need for Aggression Management skills is obvious in a world of increasing anxiety and hostility, a world where an individual like Michael McDermott enters his office and shoots to kill seven of his co-workers. We must identify the emergence of aggression, foresee the possibility of conflict, engage and prevent aggression. Anything less is not enough. A shift supervisor in Detroit talks a mechanic out of bludgeoning a co-worker. A store manager in Tucson deals with an irrational customer. A police officer in Atlanta approaches a stolen vehicle after a high-speed chase. One student hears another tell a friend he's got a pistol in his locker. Two enraged drivers race and swerve through traffic cursing one another. And up at 37,000 feet, two flight attendants struggle with an irate, slightly drunk passenger. Just these six examples remind us at a glance that aggression can erupt anywhere anytime, and seem to have *no apparent reason.*

But there is *always* a reason. Our objective in *Before Conflict* is to reinforce the theory that because aggression is everywhere in our society, everyone can benefit from having the skills and knowledge of an Aggression Manager. Who needs Aggression Management training? Well, who needs to know CPR? Some more than others, but ultimately everyone.

AGGRESSION MANAGEMENT SOLUTIONS

There are several applications of Aggression Management solutions available for managers, supervisors, educators, public service employees or anyone else who interacts with fellow workers or the public every working day.

Aggression Management Consulting

The Center for Aggression Management can integrate Aggression Management solutions within any employer's programs, procedures and polices, crisis management services, crisis response teams and effective implementation of employee assistance programs as they relate to aggression in the workplace and schools.

Aggression Management Diagnostic

What is the cost of aggression? The United Kingdom's Royal Mail has determined that the cost from "employee friction," i.e., aggression, is £247,000,000 per year. As we've pointed out, when there are aggressors in your workforce, no one else wants to be there. This causes tardiness, absenteeism and finally turnover. The cost to productivity is profound.

Aggression is no longer a mystery. Scientists have identified many causes for aggression and its corresponding violence. However, there is no aggressive behavior unless first there is aggressive thought. These thoughts stem from belief systems that support a rationale for aggression. One of the crucial advancements in know-how of recent history is the ability to convince humans to change their approach to aggression and thus aggressive reaction and behavior.

As you remember Dr. Charles Coker writing: aggression in the workplace has become an increasing problem for America and the world. Prevention and intervention are necessary if the workforce is to become safe for those of us who live and go to work every day now—and in the future. An unsafe work environment does and will continue to negatively affect productivity and profitability. This translates into real dollars and can make the difference between a company that shows a profit and one that does not. Accidents, absenteeism, turnover and low morale can all be attributed in part to aggression issues. Additionally, anxiety due to aggression can become paralyzing to the workforce.

It is therefore important for upper management to recognize that there is a cost associated with aggression, and to provide prevention and intervention strategies on an ongoing basis. To that end, the Center for Aggression Management put in place such a strategy. For bench-marking purposes the strategy process begins with a survey that reports specific aggression issues within an organization and the cost of aggression in their organization.

Aggression Management Training

In-house workshops are arranged with individual companies. Organizations can choose from a number of alternatives that can be modified to meet specific organizations' needs, such as:

- Two-Day Comprehensive Workshop—This in-depth workshop provides a comprehensive coverage of the three Arts of Aggression Management. Participants will learn all "The Arts" and be able to apply them effectively. Those who complete the course receive a Certificate of Achievement as an Aggression Manager.
- One-Day and Half-Day Workshops—Designed for employees with limited availability, these eight-hour or four-hour sessions provide a participatory learning experience in the Arts of Aggression Management.
- Four-Day Instructor's Workshop—This train-the-trainer program is intended to provide an in-house training capability for any organization. Prospective instructors take the Two-Day Comprehensive Workshop and then have two more days of intensive training and exercises including practice teaching. Upon successful completion, participants receive Instructor Certification from the center.
- Half-Day Manager's Overview—Selected decision-makers will gain a concise understanding of the basic principles and skills needed to effectively predict, prevent and defuse aggressive behavior in the workplace. The overview format enables participants to understand and evaluate the workshop's potential for wider application in their organization.

Approximately every two months, the center conducts workshops that are open to general participation.

Video-Based Training

- Interactive Video Workshop—Designed to be a half-day interactive training program. Interactivity is accomplished through the use of a workbook and/or a facilitator. This video uses examples that include office, workstation and industrial-based scenes.
- Compact Video—Designed for employee orientation, refresher, etc.—a shorter version of the above video workshop lasting approximately 26 minutes. Workbooks or facilitator's handbook does not accompany the video.

Aggression Management Mitigation

A continuation of Aggression Management consultancy and an area of increasing employer need is provided through loss control professionals, risk managers and legal consultants:

- Identifying risk and hazards and the creation of an Aggression Management Matrix
- Identifying existing controls, such as in place security and observations points, etc.
- Identifying new controls
- Preparing and presenting updated policies and procedures
- Implementation phase all of the above
- Reevaluation annually to remain current

You have read this far, and have at least a cursory idea of the tactics and techniques of Aggression Management. What is your responsibility? Remember the Mind Method—Ninjas loved knowledge. They believed knowledge was power and they practiced, practiced, practiced their knowledge. In this way the Ninjas were able to accomplish these tasks that seemed impossible with relative ease. By reading this book you have acquired the knowledge, and now you must practice, practice and practice some more until these skills become second nature to you.

Then, one day when you least expect it, you'll be thrust into a situation requiring those very special skills. And when it's over, people around you will say "I can't believe you got him calmed down—and you made it look so easy!"

I challenge you to re-examine the fine points of verbal and non-verbal persuasion, take them to heart and practice them whenever possible. Become very familiar with the Aggression Continuum. It is your template to diffuse and document aggression. Practice those personal skills like cycle breathing, slowing your heart rate and visualizing the possibility of conflict and preparing yourself with effective responses; make sure that you are not part of the problem. Like CPR, who can say when the need for Aggression Management skills will arise.

For employees in potentially perilous jobs, for law enforcement officers, public health workers, educators, postal employees and others, *you are on the front line.* I challenge you to *use* the skills you've learned herein—to manage the actions of an emerging aggressor, as well as to control the emerging aggression within yourselves. And finally, always make sure that you are part of the solution, not part of the problem.

Glossary

(An) Absolute—An objective and universal truth/rule accepted by everyone, or at least the majority, e.g., "Thou shalt not kill."

Acceptance by Association, Persuasive Tactic of—People tend to accept opinions or ideas endorsed by others they trust or admire, listen to whom they like, agree with whom they respect. *See also* Assumption of the Obvious, Because, Being Credible, Continuity, Contrast, Creating Expectation, Expanding on Perspective, False Credibility, Fears, Framing, Friends, Infectious Emotions, Invoking Spite, Limited Offer, Peer Conformity, Perception as Truth, Persuasive Tactic, Power, Projected Thinking, Reciprocity, Reduced Concession, Reducing Isolation, Sharing Secrets, and Words with Power. *Learn more about* Persuasive Tactics in "The Art of Persuasion, Pacing the Aggressor—Strategies."

Adrenaline—A hormone secreted in the adrenal gland that raises blood pressure, increases heartbeat and acts as a neurotransmitter when the body is subjected to stress or danger (*often used informally*). *See also* Adrenaline Rush.

Adrenaline Rush—The body's natural response to a situation where personal danger (perceived or real) is imminent; nature's "fight or flight" enhancer; bodily surge of the hormone adrenaline during extreme stress, which enhances heart rate, creates a hearing loss and constricts the blood vessels. *Learn more about* "Adrenaline Rush" in the "Art of Being Prepared."

Aggression—An outwardly or inwardly directed, overt or suppressed resentment either innate or resulting from continued anxiety or stress. As Aggression Managers we often identify this aggression when the aggressor ceases to cope with their anxiety or stress. To a greater degree, an unprovoked attack; forceful, attacking behavior; destructively hostile to others or to oneself. A hostile action, especially a physical or military attack, directed against another person or country, often without provocation; threatening behavior or actions; embodies everything from verbal abuse through violent behavior. This includes the subjects of Sexual Harassment, Bullying, Management-Labor Disputes, Domestic Violence Spillover, Road Rage,

Student-Teacher Conflict, Robbery, Militancy-Terrorism and Homicide. Dr. Byrnes offers these indicators of emerging aggression: 1) Not able to cope with anxiety and/or stress; 2) triggered anxiety and stress seem to mount one on another; 3) scattered or disjointed thinking; 4) becoming more distant and detached from those around us; 5) becoming fixated on our view, competitive, distrustful and self absorbed; 6) argumentative and/or belligerent; 7) use of uncustomary vulgarity or profanity; 8) sabotaging equipment; 9) planting a seed of distrust; 10) demonstrating deniable punishment behavior; 11) presenting others with ultimatums; 12) individual making threats or intimidations; 13) declaring another as an enemy; 14) interrupted communication; 15) vicious attacks on another; 16) taking self-destructive action in an attempt to destroy the enemy.

Aggression Continuum—The Center for Aggression Management's graphic depicting, in its simplest form, the three phases of aggression: the Trigger Phase, the Escalation Phase, and the Crisis Phase. An illustration of the process an aggressor experiences from the very outset of anxiety through the explosion of violence, it shows that for every incident there are pre-incidents. In its complete form the Aggression Continuum offers a template to identify aggression in others, so as to select the most effective tool(s) to diffuse the aggressor; a template to identify aggression in ourselves so that we may use the tools available to us to diffuse ourselves and a template provides a clear clinical observation for subsequent documentation. *See also* Center for Aggression Management.

Aggression Management—Individuals' use of skills to prevent aggression rather than merely react to it; used by a cross-section of individuals, they have proven to be effective in diminishing aggression and increasing productivity. *See also* Aggression Manager.

Aggression Manager—A person empowered with the skills to identify the emergence of aggression and foresee the possibility of conflict so that they may engage and prevent it. If conflict exists, the Aggression Manager also knows how to defuse aggression and, if this is not enough, the Aggression Manager knows how to effectively intervene in a way that minimizes both harm and expense. A cornerstone to being an effective Aggression Manager is the sense of responsibility to engage an emerging aggressor and defuse aggression before it becomes conflict, thereby preventing aggression. *See also* Aggression Management.

Aggressor—An individual who exhibits aggression or aggressive behavior. To a greater degree, an attacker, a person who attacks or starts a war, a fight, or an argument, often without being provoked. *See also* Aggression.

Alpha—The beginning stage of aggression, noted for anxiety and stress; first or most important part.

Analysis Paralysis—When putting too much emphasis on rational thinking or over rationalizing a situation leaves a shortage of emotions to move the body when needed.

Angle Method, Solo Intervention—Utilizing the aggressor's diminished angle of peripheral vision to the Aggression Manager's advantage. Because the aggressor is captivated by his adrenaline rush he is transfixed on his target, usually the narrow area called the victim's lifeline. *See also* Blinding Method, Mind Method, Misdirection Method, Scarf Method and Solo Intervention.

Anxiety—Feeling of worry, nervousness or agitation, often about something that is going to happen, a subject or concern that causes worry, the strong wish to do a particular thing, especially if the wish is unnecessarily strong. This anxiety can be interpreted by the brain as a threat propelling the individual into a state of fight or flight, manifested physiologically as increased heart rate, sweating, trembling, weakness and stomach or intestinal discomfort. In psychiatry, extreme apprehension: a state of intense apprehension or fear of real or imagined danger often perceived as a mental disorder.

Art of Being Prepared—The art of understanding aggression and aggressive behavior enabling an Aggression Manager the ability to effectively identify the emergence of aggression so that he/she can engage and prevent aggression. When you develop a plan to deal with aggression, institute that plan in your organization, and practice its implementation. Then, if and when aggression erupts, you can be knowledgeable, trained and practiced to manage aggression effectively and professionally. *See also* the Arts of Aggression Management, the Art of Manual Persuasion, the Art of Persuasion and the Art of Safe Escape.

Art of Manual Persuasion—The fourth art, it is the "Art" of last resort. It involves techniques used to take control of an aggressor without injuring the individual. No injury, no *basis* for a lawsuit. Manual Persuasion uses reflex pain to induce compliance. You evoke these techniques and the aggressor's reflex impulses causes him to comply.

Art of Persuasion—The process of communication and its related techniques that the Aggression Manager can use to effectively assume and maintain control over an emerging aggressor, persuading this aggressor away from perpetrating an aggressive act. *See also* the Arts of Aggression Management, the Art of Manual Persuasion, Art of Being Prepared, and the Art of Safe Escape.

Art of Safe Escape—Every incident of aggression will not end peaceably. Some individuals have already predetermined to take their confrontation to the level of physical violence, and no amount of skillful persuasion will change their mind. If "flight" becomes the final option, this is the "Art" of affecting a safe escape out of harm's way. *See also* the Arts of Aggression Management, the Art of Manual Persuasion, Art of Being Prepared, and the Art of Persuasion.

Arts of Aggression Management—The arts of employing the skills taught in Aggression Management. These human-based skills for employers and employees alike to use to prevent aggression rather than merely react to it; they have proven to be effective in diminishing aggression and increasing productivity. The Arts of Being Prepared, Persuasion, Safe Escape and Manual Persuasion are all encompassed within the Arts of Aggression Management. *See also* Aggression Management, the Art of Being Prepared, the Art of Manual Persuasion, the Art of Being Prepared, the Art of Persuasion and the Art of Safe Escape.

Assumption of the Obvious, Persuasive Tactic of—When we give people credit for knowing something they know nothing about, they generally will say nothing and allow us to believe them to be smarter or more aware than they really are. Even better, your assumption of their knowledge flatters them. *See also* Acceptance by Association, Because, Being Credible, Contrast, Continuity, Creating Expectation, Expanding on Perspective, False Credibility, Fears, Framing, Friends, Infectious Emotions, Invoking Spite, Limited Offer, Peer Conformity, Perception as Truth, Persuasive Tactic, Power, Projected Thinking, Reciprocity, Reduced Concession, Reducing Isolation, Sharing Secrets and Words with Power. *Learn more about* Persuasive Tactics in chapter 5 "The Art of Persuasion, Pacing the Aggressor—Strategies."

Auditory Exclusion—Loss of hearing due to the Adrenaline Rush.

Autocratic Persuasion—The use of authoritarian or militaristic manner to obtain results. *See also* Convincing Persuasion.

Auto Response Mode—A condition where a person, under stress, reacts without thinking due to prior training.

Barrier Signaling—A form of "Instinctive Gestures," a means of saying, "You're crossing over into my territory," a territorial response such as stepping back when someone gets too close.

Because, Persuasive Tactic of—Offering a reason, a "because," is an effective Persuasive Tactic. People need to hear a reason for a request, they respond much more favorably. *See also* Acceptance by Association, Assumption of the Obvious, Being Credible, Contrast, Continuity, Creating Expectation, Expanding on Perspective, False Credibility, Fears, Framing, Friends, Infectious Emotions, Invoking Spite, Limited Offer, Peer Conformity, Perception as Truth, Persuasive Tactic, Power, Projected Thinking, Reciprocity, Reduced Concession, Reducing Isolation, Sharing Secrets and Words with Power. *Learn more about* Persuasive Tactics in chapter 5 "The Art of Persuasion, Pacing the Aggressor—Strategies."

Behavior—Observed actions and/or reactions of an individual or group of individuals with a focus on their interrelationships. An Aggression Manager's objective is to determine an aggressor's intent through their observed behavior. *See also* Primal Aggression Continuum, Cognitive Aggression Continuum, Body Language, Adrenaline, Verbal Aggression Scale.

Being Credible, Persuasive Tactic of—Credibility is in the eye of the perceiver. Never tell another person more than he can believe; the more objective you appear, the more credibility you gain. *See also* Acceptance by Association, Assumption of the Obvious, Because, Continuity, Contrast, Creating Expectation, Expanding on Perspective, False Credibility, Fears, Framing, Friends, Infectious Emotions, Invoking Spite, Limited Offer, Peer Conformity, Perception as Truth, Persuasive Tactic, Power, Projected Thinking, Reciprocity, Reduced Concession, Reducing Isolation, Sharing Secrets and Words with Power. *Learn more about* Persuasive Tactics in chapter 5 "The Art of Persuasion, Pacing the Aggressor—Strategies."

Blading—The technique of turning ones body at a 45° angle to another person while still keeping eye contact, useful when approaching an aggressor and providing a means to get close and more intimate yet avoiding a more "direct" opportunity for confrontation.

Blinding Method, Solo Intervention—Throwing the aggressor into the "Oh God!" reflex using small non-injurious objects thrown toward the face and eyes, objects such as coins, water or non-toxic substances. Hot coffee, pencils or a lead ashtray could cause injury, which is not your objective. *See also* Angle Method, Mind Method, Misdirection Method, and Scarf Method and Solo Intervention.

Body Language—Physiological changes in the aggressor's outward appearance that others can observe. These changes are used to determine where an aggressor is on the Aggression Continuum. *See also* Primal Aggression Continuum, Cognitive Aggression Continuum, Behavior, Adrenaline, Verbal Aggression Scale.

Bulldozer, The Unmagnificent Seven—Tries to overwhelm with facts and figures; goal is to establish himself as the indispensable expert in everything; arrogant and superior in demeanor and having little regard for the knowledge and opinions of others. *See also* Unmagnificent Seven, Clam, Complainer, Exploder, Negativist, Sherman Tank, and Sniper. *Learn more about* the Universal Approaches and the Unmagnificent Seven in chapter 3, "The Arts of Aggression Management: Being Prepared."

Change-Oriented Thinkers—Look forward to and embrace change, the opportunity of an adventure. *See also* Status Quo Thinkers.

Clam, The Unmagnificent Seven—Remains silent and unresponsive to any request for ideas, suggestions, and solutions. Because the Clam keeps his feelings and emotions pent up, he can be the most dangerous of all the Unmagnificent Seven. *See also* Unmagnificent Seven, Bulldozer, Complainer, Exploder, Negativist, Sherman Tank, and Sniper. *Learn more about* the Universal Approaches and the Unmagnificent Seven in chapter 3, "The Arts of Aggression Management: Being Prepared."

Closed Questions—Also known as closed-ended questions, can be answered with a "yes" or "no"—not a good type of question to use when trying to identify the Crux of the Matter. *See also* Crux of the Matter, Open Questions, Probing Questions, Leading Questions, and Loaded Questions. *Learn more about* the Closed Questions in chapter 5 "The Art of Persuasion, Pacing the Aggressor—Strategies."

Cognitive Aggression—Thoughts or actions an aggressor takes that are deliberate and conscious (or non-conscious), manipulative in nature, to achieve and maintain an advantage over "victims." *See also* Primal Aggression Continuum, Primal Aggression, Cognitive Aggression Continuum, Non-Conscious, Victims, Violence.

Cognitive Aggression Continuum—The Cognitive Aggression Continuum describes deliberate and conscious thought that through repetition may become non-conscious. These actions enable the aggressor to achieve and maintain an advantage over "victims." For the most part an aggressor will go through both the Cognitive and Primal Aggression Continuum simultaneously. Sometimes an aggressor can transcend through the Cognitive Aggression Continuum and not yet perpetrate physical violence. In this case the Cognitive Aggression Continuum may be considered a planning phase for the aggressor. When the aggressor's thought processes have become clouded (Primal Aggression), the aggressor's violent plan will be already formulated (Cognitive Aggression). *See also* Adrenaline, Primal Aggression Continuum, Primal Aggression, Cognitive Aggression, Non-Conscious, Victims, Violence.

Community—Your community is made up of those individuals with whom you want to be seen; the individuals that you like/love/respect and you want them to like/love/respect you.

Community Policing—Where the community, the local police and the local government work together to identify and resolve crime problems.

Complainer—One of The Unmagnificent Seven, whines constantly, feels totally unappreciated and powerless to improve his condition. *See also* Unmagnificent Seven, Clam, Bulldozer, Exploder, Negativist, Sherman Tank and Sniper. *Learn more about* the Universal Approaches and The Unmagnificent Seven in chapter 3, "The Arts of Aggression Management: Being Prepared."

Compliment, Universal Approaches—When diffusing the Unmagnificent Seven, one of five Universal Approaches, the tactic of starting this encounter on a constructive note by saying something positive to an aggressor. *See also* Universal Approaches, Convince, Document, Separate and Team Productivity.

Conditioned Response—When a certain situation or circumstance arises, we respond in a certain way. The more the situation or circumstance occurs, the more automatic our response. Over time, the response becomes a habit, whether constructive or destructive, a constructive example is simulator training for airline pilots.

Continuity, Persuasive Tactic of—Once in a pattern you will continue that behavior. Predictability gives people a sense of control and comfort. *See also* Acceptance by Association, Assumption of the Obvious, Because, Being Credible, Contrast, Creating Expectation, Expanding on Perspective, False Credibility, Fears, Framing, Friends, Infectious Emotions, Invoking Spite, Limited Offer, Peer Conformity, Perception as Truth, Persuasive Tactic, Power, Projected Thinking, Reciprocity, Reduced Concession Reducing Isolation, Sharing Secrets and Words with Power. *Learn more about* Persuasive Tactics in chapter 5 "The Art of Persuasion, Pacing the Aggressor—Strategies."

Contrast, Persuasive Tactic of—When two items are relatively different from each other, we will see them as more different if placed in close proximity of each other—either in time or space. If you want something to contrast starkly, show or share them together. Bring up both issues together, at the same time. If you want to diminish the differences between two issues, share them further apart. Show one today and the other a week, month, or years from today, e.g., "The results of your actions today will have far-reaching consequences tomorrow." *See also* Acceptance by Association, Assumption of the Obvious, Because, Being Credible, Continuity, Creating

Expectation, Expanding on Perspective, False Credibility, Fears, Framing, Friends, Infectious Emotions, Invoking Spite, Limited Offer, Peer Conformity, Perception as Truth, Persuasive Tactic, Power, Projected Thinking, Reciprocity, Reduced Concession Reducing Isolation, Sharing Secrets and Words with Power. *Learn more about* Persuasive Tactics in chapter 5 "The Art of Persuasion, Pacing the Aggressor—Strategies."

Controlling Options—A strategy that enables the aggressor to select an option for action, making sure that the options offered are options acceptable to you.

Convince, Universal Approaches—When diffusing the Unmagnificent Seven, the tactic of persuading a person that his behavior is not in his own best interest. This puts him on notice that he is damaging his case, and indeed his own future with his behavior, and needs to re-examine his actions immediately. We call this "Impressment." *See also* Universal Approaches, Convincing, Document, Impressment, Separate and Team Productivity.

Convincing Persuasion—Causing the aggressor to go where you want him to go because he believes that it is in his best interests. *See also* Universal Approaches, Autocratic Persuasion, Compliment, Convince, Document, Separate and Team Productivity.

Cooling Off—Taking a break to let a heated situation cool down, a change of scenery. It can mean removing yourself from the room, leaving the aggressor alone. *See also* Suggestion, Reframing, and Triangling. *Learn more about* Suggestion in chapter 6 "The Art of Persuasion, Pacing the Aggressor—Verbal Persuasion."

Creating Expectation, Persuasive Tactic of—When someone, whom you respect or believe in, expects you to perform a task or act in a certain way, you tend to fulfill his expectations whether positive or negative. *See also* Acceptance by Association, Assumption of the Obvious, Because, Being Credible, Continuity, Contrast, Expanding on Perspective, False Credibility, Fears, Framing, Friends, Infectious Emotions, Invoking Spite, Limited Offer, Peer Conformity, Perception as Truth, Persuasive Tactic, Power, Projected Thinking, Reciprocity, Reduced Concession Reducing Isolation, Sharing Secrets and Words with Power. *Learn more about* Persuasive Tactics in chapter 5 "The Art of Persuasion, Pacing the Aggressor—Strategies."

Crisis Phase—The final phase of the Aggression Continuum, when an individual loses verbal control and then completely loses the quality of judgment, followed by the loss of physical control.

Crux of the Matter—This is the crucial point, an essential or deciding point or element that is the root to aggression. Your objective, as an Aggression

Manager is to identify the crux of aggression and reconcile it. *See also* Closed Questions, Leading Questions, Loaded Questions, Open Questions and Probing Questions. *Learn more about* the Crux of the Matter in chapter 5 "The Art of Persuasion, Pacing the Aggressor—Strategies."

Cycle Breathing—You consciously breathe in deeply through your nose, counting to four, hold to the count of two, exhale out through your mouth to the count of four, and hold to the count of two. A technique perfected by the military and law enforcement, it relaxes your body, increases blood flow and essential oxygen flow to your brain, and counteracts the effects of adrenaline. Possibly the most important tool for individuals caught in the throes of aggression.

Default Thinking—When our minds create short cuts to process the flood of input our minds receive each day. A phone call thanking you for you support over the years creates instant default thinking, which cuts to the conclusion that this is a call for a charity donation.

Deflection—Your best defensive strategy against insults, use "strip phrasing" to strip the insult of its power by moving quickly beyond it, e.g., "I hear what you are saying. However, the larger picture is . . ." *See also* Strip Phrasing.

Deliberate Expression—A type of non-verbal feedback that includes all types of conscious or semi-conscious facial expressions. There are expressions, like a smile, that we believe that we can manipulate. But these smiles appear "plastic" because those parts of a smile tied to the *autonomic nervous system* (ANS) like the wrinkling below our eyes; the crow's feet indications and a subtle dip in the brow are absent. *See also* Deliberate Gesticulation, Instinctive Expression and Instinctive Gesticulation.

Deliberate Gesticulation—A type of non-verbal feedback including all conscious gestures, mannerisms and posture, primarily using hands and arms to reinforce a verbal message. *See also* Deliberate Expression, Instinctive Expression and Instinctive Gesticulation.

Deniable Punishment Behavior—This is where an aggressor punishes his victim with sarcasm so that later he can say that he was just kidding. This is the action of a Sniper. *See also* Sniper.

Depersonalization—During the Escalation Phase a person begins to think of the victim as an object. Once the victim is thought of as an object it becomes easier for an aggressor to continue up the Aggression Continuum.

Disconcerts—Phrases that may disrupt an aggressor's thought processes when he is in a state of high anxiety. Normal thought processes are already impaired due to the aggressor's adrenaline rush. Because the aggressor's focus is impaired, he is unable to thoroughly think rationally. The Aggression Manager may make a statement that causes the aggressor to respond in a way that encourages him to leave or cease his aggression.

Document, Universal Approaches—You can acknowledge the Unmagnificent person for his specific personality type by documenting and discussing previous incidents, but doing so in a neutral, reflective and constructive manner. Recommend that prior incidents be documented in writing. *See also* Universal Approaches, Compliment, Convince, Separate and Team Productivity.

Documentation—The paper trail; policies differ from organization to organization but know what to document, don't delay, interview all the witnesses, be objective, organize chronologically and tell the truth.

Emotional Weighting—An aggressor begins to weight a normal discussion with his emotions trying to trigger and incite your emotions, moving you from your logic and reason to his emotions, where he wins.

Empathy—Derived from the Latin "*em*" a prefix that means "put one's self into," and the Greek "*pathy*" for "suffering" or "feeling;" a demonstration of understanding the plight or perceived injuries suffered by the aggressor.

Escalation Phase—This is the second phase of the Aggression Continuum; when an individual can no longer cope with triggered anxiety and/or stress, as one trigger accumulates upon another creating mounting anxiety.

Expanding on Perspective, Persuasive Tactic of—Once an individual has announced that he is taking a position on any issue or point of view, he will strongly defend that belief regardless of its accuracy even in the face of overwhelming evidence to the contrary. An Aggression Manager may find it easier to convince an aggressor that he is not an aggressor than it is to convince him not to act aggressively. *See also* Acceptance by Association, Assumption of the Obvious, Because, Being Credible, Continuity, Contrast, Creating Expectation, False Credibility, Fears, Framing, Friends, Infectious Emotions, Invoking Spite, Limited Offer, Peer Conformity, Perception as Truth, Persuasive Tactics, Power, Projected Thinking, Reciprocity, Reduced Concession, Reducing Isolation, Sharing Secrets and Words with Power. *Learn more about* Persuasive Tactics in chapter 5 "The Art of Persuasion, Pacing the Aggressor—Strategies."

Exploder, The Unmagnificent Seven—Exhibits mood swings between calm and loud, temperamental outbursts; full of insults and name-calling; goal is to silence the competition and intimidate them, and others, to be submissive. *See also* Unmagnificent Seven, Bulldozer, Clam, Complainer, Negativist, Sherman Tank and Sniper. *Learn more about* the Universal Approaches and the Unmagnificent Seven in chapter 3, "The Arts of Aggression Management: Being Prepared."

Externally Motivated—A person who is influenced greatly by advice and what they perceive as the opinions and wishes of those whom they respect. *See also* Community and Internally Motivated.

False Credibility, Persuasive Tactic of—Humans tend to like products, services or suggestions that are endorsed by others they like or respect, whether the "others" are credible or not. People tend to agree to suggestions that will be perceived as acceptable by the majority of other people or a majority of their "community." *See also* Acceptance by Association, Assumption of the Obvious, Because, Being Credible, Continuity, Contrast, Creating Expectation, Expanding on Perspective, Fears, Framing, Friends, Infectious Emotions, Invoking Spite, Limited Offer, Peer Conformity, Perception as Truth, Persuasive Tactic, Power, Projected Thinking, Reciprocity, Reduced Concession, Reducing Isolation, Sharing Secrets and Words with Power. *Learn more about* Persuasive Tactics in chapter 5 "The Art of Persuasion, Pacing the Aggressor—Strategies."

Fears, Persuasive Tactic of—By focusing on things that cause us fear, anguish and anxiety, we give that fear, anguish and anxiety power. Be aware of the things that cause anxiety but focus on the things that produce solutions. *See also* Acceptance by Association, Assumption of the Obvious, Because, Being Credible, Continuity, Contrast, Creating Expectation, Expanding on Perspective, False Credibility, Framing, Friends, Infectious Emotions, Invoking Spite, Limited Offer, Peer Conformity, Perception as Truth, Persuasive Tactic, Power, Projected Thinking, Reciprocity, Reduced Concession, Reducing Isolation, Sharing Secrets and Words with Power. *Learn more about* Persuasive Tactics in chapter 5 "The Art of Persuasion, Pacing the Aggressor—Strategies."

Framing, Persuasive Tactic of—people don't like to be told what to do, so this tactic is about "Framing" a statement to create a desired result, e.g., "I could tell you that you are making a mistake, but I won't. You want to figure it out for yourself." We like to think that each great idea is ours and, when we have some great revelation or insight, it is entirely our own. *See also* Acceptance by Association, Assumption of the Obvious, Because, Being Credible, Continuity, Contrast, Creating Expectation, Expanding on Perspective, False Credibility, Fears, Friends, Infectious Emotions, Invoking Spite, Limited Offer, Peer Conformity, Perception as Truth, Persuasive Tactic, Power, Projected Thinking, Reciprocity, Reduced Concession, Reducing Isolation, Sharing Secrets and Words with Power. *Learn more about* Persuasive Tactics in chapter 5 "The Art of Persuasion, Pacing the Aggressor—Strategies."

Freezing—Defined by the "motionless" response to a threat that overcomes the person's ability to respond. According to Lt. Col. Dave Grossman (Army Ret.), typically occurs with a heart rate greater than 175 bpm. The person becomes too scared to move and because of this inability to move—becomes a victim. See Primal Aggression Continuum, Cognitive Aggression Continuum, Adrenaline.

Friends, Persuasive Tactic of—It is important to be perceived by the aggressor as a friend if you are to be successful in the persuasion process because, when someone you like and trust asks you to do something, you want to do it. *See also* Acceptance by Association, Assumption of the Obvious, Because, Being Credible, Continuity, Contrast, Creating Expectation, Expanding on Perspective, False Credibility, Fears, Framing, Infectious Emotions, Invoking Spite, Limited Offer, Peer Conformity, Perception as Truth, Persuasive Tactic, Power, Projected Thinking, Reciprocity, Reduced Concession, Reducing Isolation, Sharing Secrets and Words with Power. *Learn more about* Persuasive Tactics in chapter 5 "The Art of Persuasion, Pacing the Aggressor—Strategies."

Get Real—When something of magnitude occurs, the Aggression Manager must remain focused. Often when this "aggressive moment" occurs, it may cause the Aggression Manager to go into a form of shock and lose their ability to cope with the situation. The Get Real technique enables the Aggression Manager to be as lucid as possible in the aggressive moment, using all of the "Arts" to respond in the most effective way. This technique prevents a form of shock in potentially dangerous situations. The Aggression Manager who is "in the moment" retains calm objectivity enabling him or her to maximize effectiveness through cycle breathing. Note: If the Aggression Manager doesn't Get Real, they may go into the "Oh God!" reflex and be unable to prevent an act of aggression.

Global Thinkers—Global Thinkers see the big picture and often do not want to get involved with details. They tend to get bogged down by details.

Hypervigilance—A state of heightened alert that an aggressor initiates in the Escalation Phase and is in full effect during the Crisis Phase. *See also* Primal Aggression Continuum, Cognitive Aggression Continuum, Adrenaline.

Impressment—A strategy that convinces the aggressor to come with you along a course of action because it is in his best interests—and, *if possible*, have him believe that it is his idea. *See also* Universal Approaches, Convince, Convincing, Document, Separate and Team Productivity.

Infectious Emotions, Persuasive Tactic of—Emotions are infectious: anger, panic, fear or unruffled calm. This is where an Aggression Manager uses his skills to prevent negative emotions from growing within an aggressor or himself and encourages the spread of his own calm, unruffled demeanor. *See also* Acceptance by Association, Assumption of the Obvious, Because, Being Credible, Continuity, Contrast, Creating Expectation, Expanding on Perspective, False Credibility, Fears, Framing, Friends, Invoking Spite, Limited Offer, Peer Conformity, Perception as Truth, Persuasive Tactic, Power, Projected Thinking, Reciprocity, Reduced Concession, Reducing Isolation, Sharing Secrets and Words with Power. *Learn more about* Persuasive Tactics in chapter 5 "The Art of Persuasion, Pacing the Aggressor—Strategies."

Instinctive Expression—A type of non-verbal communication, which are far more reliable because they are tied to the *autonomic nervous system* (ANS) and are therefore instinctive; including unconscious facial expressions such as a smile or flushing or blanching of facial coloring. There are expressions, like a natural smile, that we believe that we can manipulate. But these smiles appear "plastic" because those parts of a smile tied to the *autonomic nervous system* (ANS) like the wrinkling below our eyes, the crow's feet indications and a subtle dip in the brow are absent. *See also* Deliberate Expression, Deliberate Gesticulation and Instinctive Gesticulation.

Instinctive Gesticulation—A type of non-verbal communication which includes unconscious gestures such as crossing ones arms or legs or covering ones mouth with a hand when one is lying. (This, of course, does not mean that everyone crossing their arms is lying.) *See also* Deliberate Expression, Deliberate Gesticulation and Instinctive Expression.

Internally Motivated—A person who does not readily respond to demands, looks for decisions and is motivated by internal measurements. They tend to think others are wrong when they disagree with them.

Intimidation—The most advanced, most serious escalation of verbal aggression in the Escalation Phase of the Aggression Continuum. With intimidation and threats, the aggressor is at the threshold of the Crisis Phase.

Invoking Spite, Persuasive Tactic of—Use of people's resentment toward being thought of as inferior in any way to get an aggressor to do what you want/need him to do, e.g., "You may not understand what I am about to tell you." *See also* Acceptance by Association, Assumption of the Obvious, Because, Being Credible, Continuity, Contrast, Creating Expectation, Expanding on Perspective, False Credibility, Fears, Framing, Friends, Infectious Emotions, Limited Offer, Peer Conformity, Perception as Truth, Persuasive Tactic, Power, Projected Thinking, Reciprocity, Reduced Concession, Reducing Isolation, Sharing Secrets and Words with Power. *Learn more about* Persuasive Tactics in chapter 5 "The Art of Persuasion, Pacing the Aggressor—Strategies."

Leading Questions—Are questions that often provide our own conclusions in the form of a question, enabling the responding individual (the aggressor) to confirm that conclusion. They do not help the Aggression Manager identify what is the Crux of the Matter. Once the Crux of the Matter has been determined, they help the Aggression Manager validate the Crux of the Matter and move the aggressor in a direction the Aggression Manager wishes them to go. *See also* Crux of the Matter, Closed Questions, Loaded Questions, Open Questions and Probing Questions. *Learn more about* the Crux of the Matter in chapter 5 "The Art of Persuasion, Pacing the Aggressor— Strategies."

Lifeline—The vital area of the body, when two lines are drawn from the corners of our eyes down our torso to intersect at the groin; the area contains 85% of all the body's vital organs and is instinctively an aggressor's primary strike zone.

Limited Offer, Persuasive Tactic of—People tend to place higher values on items that are limited in quantity; the harder it is to attain something, the greater the value placed on it, e.g., "You worked hard to gain this position, why take the risk of losing it?" *See also* Acceptance by Association, Assumption of the Obvious, Because, Being Credible, Continuity, Contrast, Creating Expectation, Expanding on Perspective, False Credibility, Fears, Framing, Friends, Infectious Emotions, Invoking Spite, Peer Conformity, Perception as Truth, Persuasive Tactic, Power, Projected Thinking, Reciprocity, Reduced Concession, Reducing Isolation, Sharing Secrets and Words with Power. *Learn more about* Persuasive Tactics in chapter 5 "The Art of Persuasion, Pacing the Aggressor—Strategies."

Linear Thinkers—Linear Thinkers love details and seldom become bored with specifics. *See also* Global Thinkers.

Loaded Questions—Never a good type of question as they incriminate or belittle the aggressor, forcing him to admit he is at fault, or they insult him. *See also* Crux of the Matter, Closed Questions, Leading Questions, Open Questions and Probing Questions. *Learn more about* the Crux of the Matter in chapter 5 "The Art of Persuasion, Pacing the Aggressor—Strategies."

Loss of Physical Control—At the top of the Crisis Phase, the process when an aggressor losses physical control of his actions. The aggressor is very near violence.

Loss of Verbal Control—At the beginning of the Crisis Phase, the process an aggressor goes through as he loses verbal control. An example is the aggressor's speech becomes disjointed and stops before losing control.

LPA—Least Possible Applause, showing disapproval by demonstrating no reaction at all to unacceptable behavior.

Mammalian Brain or Limbic System—Also referred to as mid-brain, the part of the brain that is the source of emotion, senses and nonverbal communication. *See also* Primal Aggression Continuum, Cognitive Aggression Continuum, Adrenaline, Thinking Brain, Reptilian Brain.

Maslow's Hierarchy of Needs—A pyramid describing mankind's five basic needs groupings from the basic physical needs up the pyramid to the highest level of the self-actualization needs.

Mind Method, Solo Intervention—Arming oneself with knowledge and then it's practice, practice, practice, these skills until they become second nature. Knowledge and practice is very enabling for an Aggression Manager and is one of the corner stones to Aggression Management. *See also* Angle Method, Blinding Method, Misdirection Method and Solo Intervention.

Misdirection Method, Solo Intervention—Giving the impression, physically and/or mentally, that we are going one direction, while in fact we are going another. *See also* Angle Method, Blinding Method, Mind Method, Scarf Method and Solo Intervention.

Mounting Anxiety—Anxiety that occurs when an individual stops coping, found within the Escalation Phase and is verified by changes in the aggressor's behavior, body language and interpersonal communications. *See also* Anxiety.

Negativist, The Unmagnificent Seven—Says no to every suggestion, is never happy, wants everyone to be as miserable as he is. *See also* Unmagnificent Seven, Bulldozer, Clam, Complainer, Exploder, Sherman Tank and Sniper. *Learn more about* the Universal Approaches and the Unmagnificent Seven in chapter 3 "The Arts of Aggression Management: Being Prepared."

NIOSH—The National Institute for Occupational Safety and Health.

Non-Conscious Aggression—An automatic action or thought process of an aggressor. The aggressor has learned this behavior, which has usually been reinforced by victim's acceptance, become automatic thoughts or actions that aid in maintaining an advantage and control over a victim or victims.

Non-Plus—A term used to describe being perceived as contributing no emotional input to a situation or issue, appearing completely neutral.

Non-Verbal Leakage—A form of Mounting Anxiety that indicates the possibility of the aggressor attempting to deceive the Aggression Manager; aggressive signals "leak" out through an aggressor's body language and behavior; such as crossing ones arms or legs as if to keep the truth from spilling out versus the use of free, natural gestures when telling the truth.

Non-Verbal (Manual) Pacing—A technique used to persuade an aggressor away from an aggressive act through the use of corresponding body language and behavior. This technique reflects the aggressor's behavior and communication patterns, such as breathing, blinking, crossing arms or legs, etc. Once the Aggression Manager feels a connection, he or she can stop mirroring the aggressor's body language and move into a more calm, relaxed postures and non-verbal signals thereby reassuring the aggressor of the Aggression Manager's non-threatening role. This allows the Aggression Manager to open the door toward influencing the aggressor's actions and thought processes.

"Oh God!" Reflex—Triggers shock and surprise, the act buys a half second to a second and a half to escape, is used in Solo Intervention techniques tossing small objects, such as paperclips or coins, at an aggressor just before an expected physical attack not to harm him, but to distract him, which triggers shock and surprise. You might also look over his shoulder and yell, "Grab him!" The aggressor will usually react reflexively by looking over his shoulder or by spinning around to meet the new threat from behind giving you a chance to escape. *See also* Angle Method, Blinding Method, Mind Method, Misdirection Method, Scarf Method and Solo Intervention.

Omega (In the context of Aggression Management)—The final stage of the Aggression Continuum, indicative of violence; the end, or the last thing in a series.

Open Questions—Also known as open-ended questions; what, why, when questions needing explanations and are not "yes" or "no" answers; a good type of question to offer to an aggressor to get to the Crux of the Matter. *See also* Crux of the Matter, Closed Questions, Leading Questions, Loaded questions and Probing Questions. *Learn more about* the Crux of the Matter in chapter 5 "The Art of Persuasion, Pacing the Aggressor—Strategies."

Pacing—The act of mirroring an aggressor's actions, such as crossing your legs or arms just as he has done. Also includes emulating posture and speech patterns. As you continue to talk with your aggressor you would uncross your arms and place them at your side, then your legs; as he moves more to your cadence he will begin to relax and agree more and more with what you are saying.

Paraphrasing—Repeating the aggressor's words using tone of voice and body language to change intent; a way to rephrase and simplify, to restate something using other words, especially in order to make it simpler or shorter.

Parrot Phrasing—Exactly repeating an aggressor's words using the same tone.

Peer Conformity, Persuasive Tactic of—People tend to agree to ideas or proposals they perceive as acceptable to the majority of others in their peer group, as an example, "I'm sure you're proud that your work team has a record of zero claims over the last five years. And everyone is working so hard to continue this excellent record." *See also* Acceptance by Association, Assumption of the Obvious, Because, Being Credible, Continuity, Contrast, Creating Expectation, Expanding on Perspective, False Credibility, Fears, Framing, Friends, Infectious Emotions, Invoking Spite, Limited Offer, Perception as Truth, Persuasive Tactic, Power, Projected Thinking, Reciprocity, Reduced Concession, Reducing Isolation, Sharing Secrets and Words with Power. *Learn more about* Persuasive Tactics in chapter 5 "The Art of Persuasion, Pacing the Aggressor—Strategies."

Perception as Truth, Persuasive Tactic of—What each person perceives it to be. One way someone knows you're telling the truth is that you believe the same thing he does, or come to the same conclusion. If you agree with him, then you're also right and are speaking the truth. *See also* Acceptance by Association, Assumption of the Obvious, Because, Being Credible, Continuity, Contrast, Creating Expectation, Expanding on Perspective, False Credibility, Fears, Framing, Friends, Infectious Emotions, Invoking Spite, Limited Offer, Peer Conformity, Perception as Truth, Persuasive Tactic, Power, Projected Thinking, Reciprocity, Reduced Concession, Reducing Isolation, Sharing Secrets and Words with Power. *Learn more about* Persuasive Tactics in chapter 5 "The Art of Persuasion, Pacing the Aggressor—Strategies."

Perception Process—Five filters that a message goes through after it leaves the sender/Aggression Manager before it reaches an aggressor's mind as a complete communication.

Persona of Certainty—The quality of quiet confidence an Aggression Manager possesses when he or she has the skills and competencies of Aggression Management; although they may make mistakes, they know that they can and will work through any obstacle(s).

Persuasive Tactics—In this age of information overload, we are bombarded with data and information; to be able to cope with this overload, we create mental shortcuts that become very compelling to us, e.g., a phone caller thanks us for our previous purchase, we know that this is probably a sales organization asking us to purchase something. Our automatic shortcut response may be to thank this person for their call and hang up. As an Aggression Manager we may effectively use Persuasive Tactics with an aggressor to persuade them in a particular direction—away from an aggressive act. They may, however, be used against us, so our objective is to understand and utilize them in two ways: 1) to not be manipulated by them and, 2) to persuade the aggressor away from an aggressive act. *See also* Acceptance by Association, Assumption of the Obvious, Because, Being Credible, Continuity, Contrast, Creating Expectation, Expanding on Perspective, False Credibility, Fears, Framing, Friends, Infectious Emotions, Invoking Spite, Limited Offer, Peer Conformity, Perception as Truth, Power, Projected Thinking, Reciprocity, Reduced Concession, Reducing Isolation, Sharing Secrets, Words with Power. *Learn more about* Persuasive Tactics in chapter 5 "The Art of Persuasion, Pacing the Aggressor—Strategies."

Physiological Engineering—Engineering the body to create and manage an aggressor's reflex pain, used in the Art of Manual Persuasion, the "Art" of last resort. *See also* the Art of Persuasion.

Physiological Feedback—Feedback provided by the body itself such as shallow and rapid breathing, sweating, constricted pupils, a red face and prominent veins. This type of feedback is tied more directly to the *autonomic nervous system* (ANS). Consequently this feedback is far more difficult for an aggressor to manipulate and it is therefore a more reliable aggression indicator.

Post-Traumatic Stress Disorder (PTSD)—What used to be called "battle fatigue," when people suffer, sometimes a lifetime, from the after effects of war or a traumatic or sentinel event. *See also* Sentinel Event.

Power, Persuasive Tactic of—People exercise power over other people to the degree that those exercising power are perceived as having greater authority, strength, or expertise. *See also* Acceptance by Association, Assumption of the Obvious, Because, Being Credible, Continuity, Contrast, Creating Expectation, Expanding on Perspective, False Credibility, Fears, Framing, Friends, Infectious Emotions, Invoking Spite, Limited Offer, Peer Conformity, Perception as Truth, Persuasive Tactic, Projected Thinking, Reciprocity, Reduced Concession, Reducing Isolation, Sharing Secrets and Words with Power.

Predator's Stare—The aggressor's holding mechanism, the objective is to get and hold the victim's attention and evoke fear.

Primal Aggression—Physiological (chemical-neurological) actions the body takes to preserve and protect itself. *See also* Cognitive Aggression.

Primal Aggression Continuum—The Primal Aggression Continuum reflects the physiological (chemical and neurological) actions the body takes to preserve and protect itself. These actions are exposed when an individual feels endangered or threatened, either physically or emotionally. Adrenaline, one of the primal of human chemicals, kicks in triggering of the "fight or flight" mode that also causes physiological reactions that are detected through behavior, body language and Verbal Aggression Scale. At the top of the Primal Aggression Continuum is actual, physical violence. *See also* Adrenaline, Violence, Cognitive Aggression Continuum, Primal Aggression, Cognitive Aggression, Behavior, Body language, Verbal Aggression Scale.

Probing Questions—Questions that are often follow-ups to initial Open Questions in that they delve deeper into the issues; a good type of question to get to the Crux of the Matter. *See also* Crux of the Matter, Closed Questions, Leading Questions, Loaded Questions and Open Questions. *Learn more about* the Crux of the Matter in the Art of Persuasion, Pacing the Aggressor—Strategies.

Projected Thinking, Persuasive Tactic of—Our minds tend to perceive what they are trained to perceive. People tend to project their views on reality so that reality changes to become what they project. *See also* Acceptance by Association, Assumption of the Obvious, Because, Being Credible, Continuity, Contrast, Creating Expectation, Expanding on Perspective, False Credibility, Fears, Framing, Friends, Infectious Emotions, Invoking Spite, Limited Offer, Peer Conformity, Perception as Truth, Persuasive Tactic, Power, Reciprocity, Reduced Concession, Reducing Isolation, Sharing Secrets and Words with Power. *Learn more about* Persuasive Tactics in chapter 5 "The Art of Persuasion, Pacing the Aggressor—Strategies."

Proxemics—A term to describe the distance one person likes to maintain between himself and another person. The study of the distance individuals prefer to maintain between each other in social interaction and how this separation is significant. A critical aspect of being an Aggression Manager is the ability to engage an aggressor effectively, not only by the words, but also through manual or non-verbal pacing enabling persuasion of the aggressor away from a aggressive act.

Questioning (questioning your authority)—The beginning of the Verbal Aggression Scale where the aggressor begins challenging authority. For example he may ask, "Who are you to tell me to do that?" *See also* Primal Aggression Continuum, Cognitive Aggression Continuum, Verbal Aggression Scale, Refusing, Intimidation, Questioning.

Receptors—The five senses: hearing, seeing, touching, smelling, and tasting; in other words, how we take our information in.

Reciprocity, Persuasive Tactic of—When someone gives you something of perceived value, you immediately respond with the desire to give something back—often something of greater value. *See also* Acceptance by Association, Assumption of the Obvious, Because, Being Credible, Continuity, Contrast, Creating Expectation, Expanding on Perspective, False Credibility, Fears, Framing, Friends, Infectious Emotions, Invoking Spite, Limited Offer, Peer Conformity, Perception as Truth, Persuasive Tactic, Power, Projected Thinking, Reduced Concession, Reducing Isolation, Sharing Secrets and Words with Power. *Learn more about* Persuasive Tactics in chapter 5 "The Art of Persuasion, Pacing the Aggressor—Strategies."

Reduced Concession, Persuasive Tactic of—People tend to concede to a smaller demand, if they have just turned down a much greater demand. *See also* Acceptance by Association, Assumption of the Obvious, Because, Being Credible, Continuity, Contrast, Creating Expectation, Expanding on Perspective, False Credibility, Fears, Framing, Friends, Infectious Emotions, Invoking Spite, Limited Offer, Peer Conformity, Perception as Truth, Persuasive Tactic, Power, Projected Thinking, Reciprocity, Reducing Isolation, Sharing Secrets and Words with Power. *Learn more about* Persuasive Tactics in chapter 5 "The Art of Persuasion, Pacing the Aggressor—Strategies."

Reducing Isolation, Persuasive Tactic of—Humans are social creatures by nature; they crave contact with others. In moments of uncertainty or danger, resist the desire to isolate yourself and seek out friends. *See also* Acceptance by Association, Assumption of the Obvious, Because, Being Credible, Continuity, Contrast, Creating Expectation, Expanding on Perspective, False Credibility, Fears, Framing, Friends, Infectious Emotions, Invoking Spite, Limited Offer, Peer Conformity, Perception as Truth, Persuasive Tactic, Power, Projected Thinking, Reciprocity, Reduced Concession, Sharing Secrets and Words with Power. *Learn more about* Persuasive Tactics in chapter 5 "The Art of Persuasion, Pacing the Aggressor—Strategies."

Reframing—A technique used to enhance an aggressor's quality of judgment; it helps to restore dignity after the aggressor has taken an undignified action. Reframing allows the Aggression Manager to use his or her verbal skills to soften what an aggressor did, removing some of the sting, it suggests a more positive or more honorable motive for an individual to have acted aggressively. "Maybe the real reason you've acted this way is that your own standards of quality were frustrated by the rush we've been working under." Another technique for an Aggression Manager to use in the prevention of an aggressive act. *See also* Cooling Off, Suggestion and Triangling.

Refusing (refusing to comply with instruction)—This point on the Verbal Aggression Scale where an aggressor refuses to do what is asked of him.

For example, "No, I won't do . . ." *See also* Primal Aggression Continuum, Cognitive Aggression Continuum, Verbal Aggression Scale, Refusing, Intimidation, Questioning.

Reptilian Brain (brain-stem)—Provides only basic primal instincts and reactions to threats, hunger, fear, environment (territory), etc. *See also* Primal Aggression Continuum, Cognitive Aggression Continuum, Adrenaline, Mammalian Brain and Thinking Brain.

Scarf Method, Solo Intervention—The use of illusion to accomplish a desired result, e.g., by hiring a plainclothes police officer or security person to sit outside your door the aggressor will be under the illusion that this is just another individual waiting for an appointment—not a trained professional prepared to take control at a moment's notice. *See also* Angle Method, Blinding Method, Mind Method, Misdirection Method and Solo Intervention.

Seed of Distrust, Planting a—A partial truth, outright cognitive aggression at the fourth level in the Escalation Phase; a technique used throughout our world, maybe because folks do not know how aggressive it is, that it is outright, overt aggression; If someone went to your "community" and spoke about you by saying: "You know Jane. I don't know if I can still trust her. I don't know why, I just don't feel comfortable around her anymore." I have just planted the *seed of distrust*. This insidious seed will grow like weeds in a garden. Partial truth can be far more detrimental than complete truth. We believe that if more individuals understood that they were being overtly aggressive, they may be less likely to use this behavior. Also known as Sniping. *See also* Deniable Punishment Behavior, Sniper and Sniping.

Sentinel Event—A phrase used in health care; an occurrence when an individual responds normally to an abnormal event (such as witnessing a murder) yet considers his response as abnormal and often finds himself unable to cope. *See also* Post-Traumatic Stress Disorder (PTSD).

Separate, Universal Approaches—A strategy to remove an aggressor from his crowd of admirers. It might be easier to remove the crowd from the aggressor than to remove the aggressor from the crowd. *See also* Universal Approaches, Compliment, Convince, Document and Team Productivity.

Setting Limits—A technique of controlling options. You offer the option you want them to take (with reasons) and the option with the consequence of *not* taking it. Options must be clearly stated to the aggressor and reasonable.

Sharing Secrets, Persuasive Tactic of—People love secrets and love to be included; when you share a secret, you gain a great deal of trust from your listeners. *See also* Acceptance by Association, Assumption of the Obvious,

Because, Being Credible, Continuity, Contrast, Creating Expectation, Expanding on Perspective, False Credibility, Fears, Framing, Friends, Infectious Emotions, Invoking Spite, Limited Offer, Peer Conformity, Perception as Truth, Persuasive Tactic, Power, Projected Thinking, Reciprocity, Reduced Concession, Reducing Isolation and Words with Power. *Learn more about* Persuasive Tactics in chapter 5 "The Art of Persuasion, Pacing the Aggressor—Strategies."

Sherman Tank, The Unmagnificent Seven—Enjoys confrontation; needs to prove himself right; often uses physical presence, persona or personality to intimidate others. *See also* Unmagnificent Seven, Bulldozer, Clam, Complainer, Exploder, Negativist and Sniper. *Learn more about* the Universal Approaches and the Unmagnificent Seven in chapter 3 "The Arts of Aggression Management: Being Prepared."

SHRM—Society for Human Resource Management.

Smoothing—Using suggestion to recall past, more positive feelings; can cause a calming effect on the individual as he searches his memory.

Sniper, The Unmagnificent Seven—Undermines authority and morale with criticism behind ones back; uses jokes and sarcasm to cover sniping. Sometimes a partial truth is used; it is important to note that a partial truth is more dangerous than a total lie. Also referred to as Deniable Punishment Behavior on the Cognitive Aggression Continuum, when an aggressor can use sniping and later deny it as a joke. *See also* Unmagnificent Seven, Bulldozer, Clam, Complainer, Deniable Punishment Behavior, Exploder, Negativist and Sherman Tank. *Learn more about* the Universal Approaches and the Unmagnificent Seven in chapter 3 "The Arts of Aggression Management: Being Prepared."

Sniping—The act of undermining authority and morale, planting a Seed of Distrust in someone's community. *See also* Community, Deniable Punishment Behavior, Seed of Distrust and Sniper.

Socially Toxic—Students coming from a poverty-ridden, drug infested, high crime neighborhoods may become Socially Toxic.

Solo Intervention—An intervention designed so you can remove yourself as a target, predicated on the effective application of actions associated with the "Oh God!" reflex. Some of the different intervention types include: the Angle Method, the Blinding Method, the Mind Method, the Misdirection Method, and the Scarf Method. Only to be used when Team Intervention is not available or the need for intervention was not predicted. *See also* Angle Method, Blinding Method, Mind Method, Misdirection Method, Scarf Method and "Solo Intervention."

Split Second Pause—A short pause, planted in the behavior of the Aggression Manager by the Aggression Manager, for that instance of aggression when you have not performed "Stress Inoculation," this pause will give you time to consider what's happening to you, enabling you to respond effectively and professionally—and win!

Status Quo thinkers—Status Quo thinkers prefer things as they have always been, they are upset by change. *See also* Change-Oriented Thinkers.

Stress—Strain felt by somebody, mental, emotional or physical strain caused, for example, by anxiety of overwork. It may cause such symptoms as raised blood pressure or lack of energy. Found in the Trigger Phase of the Aggression Continuum, when an individual starts not coping with their stress or anxiety, they enter the Escalation Phase. *See also* Anxiety, Adrenaline.

Stress Inoculation—When you visually implant a type, or incident of aggression and its response so that, when and if that particular aggression occurs, you will be prepared for it; a preparation to prevent the "Oh God!" reflex.

Strike Zone—The physical strike zone is within a line between the eyes and groin (lifeline). This is the area the aggressor will instinctively focus on as a potential area of vulnerability

Strip Phrasing—Moving beyond a comment or insult almost as if you didn't hear it thereby removing the "sting," power or energy of the comment, insult or question. Also see "deflection." This usually disempowers the aggressor's insult and springboards you in the direction you wish the aggressor to go. *See also* Deflection.

Suggestion—Is the strategy that plants an idea you want planted in the aggressor's mind. *See also* Cooling Off, Reframing and Triangling.

Tachypsychia—A distortion that occurs when your mind speeds up to cope with an aggressive moment and it causes our perception of that event to seem as though it were in slow motion.

Target Glancing—When an attacker takes his eyes from the victim's face and begins looking at intended strike areas, typically the area called the "lifeline." *See also* Lifeline.

Team Intervention—Using pre-arranged techniques similar to those employed in Solo Intervention, but with a team approach; you have the advantage of safety in numbers, even one more person can make the aggression situation twice as safe, it promotes professionalism, a team looks more professional and an aggressor is more likely to respond constructively if he is approached by a professional looking team; a team will support the Aggression Manager in the event of litigation. What do team members become? Built-in witnesses for the Aggression Manager. *See also* Solo Intervention.

Team Productivity, Universal Approaches—This answers the question, "How can we work together as a team to be more productive?" This is essential because it ties all the Universal Approaches together. It says that you, the Aggression Manager, care and respect this person enough to help him work through this process resulting in better productivity for all involved. *See also* Universal Approaches, Compliment, Convince, Document and Separate.

Thinking Brain—Thinking Brain or Cerebral Cortex (an oversimplification for the purposes of Aggression Management instruction)—provides "conscious thought" and is different from Mammalian Brain or Limbic System and the Reptilian Brain or Brain Stem. *See also* Primal Aggression Continuum, Cognitive Aggression Continuum, Adrenaline, Mammalian Brain, Reptilian Brain.

Threat—You will read, in this book, many references to the word *threat*. It is the feeling of being threatened and the ability to cope with that threat which denotes the initiation of aggression. (A potential aggressor channels his appraisal into some form of coping—from the Middle French *couper*; to strike or cut. The strength of the reaction is a direct function of the value of the threat and the degree of certainty that the threat will thwart an objective or a goal. Adapted from Pierce J. Howard, Ph.D., *The Owner's Manual for the Brain, Everyday Applications from Mind-Brain Research.*

Total Loss of Judgment—In the Crisis Phase just before the lose of physical control. The aggressor has a total loss of judgment. He is no longer thinking rationally and is rapidly moving toward violence.

Triangling—A technique used to deploy Suggestion; its constructive purpose is to deflects an aggressor's anger toward an abstract idea. The triangle has three sides, the aggressor, the abstract idea and you, the Aggression Manager. Triangling is also illustrated in its destructive form in the Cognitive Aggression Continuum. *See also* Cooling Off, Reframing and Suggestion.

Trigger—Found initially in the Trigger Phase of the Aggression Continuum. In the Perception Process these are persons, events, situations and objects—the stimuli that color the aggressor's perceptions.

Trigger Phase—First phase of the Aggression Continuum, the explosion(s) of anxiety.

Tunnel Vision—When peripheral vision reduces down to transfix on a threatening focal point.

Umbrella of Trust—The umbrella under which you must perform your repertoire of persuasive skills and talents.

Universal Approaches—A constructive approach, a template to assist in selecting the right words when working with one of the Unmagnificent Seven. The five Universal Approaches are: Compliment, Convince, Document, Separate and Team Productivity. *See also* Compliment, Convince, Document, Separate and Team Productivity. *Learn more about* the Universal Approaches and the Unmagnificent Seven in chapter 3 "The Arts of Aggression Management: Being Prepared."

Unmagnificent Seven—Seven basic types of troublesome and potentially aggressive personalities. These personalities include: the Bulldozer, the Clam, the Complainer, the Exploder, the Negativist, the Sherman Tank and the Sniper. *See also* Bulldozer, Clam, Complainer, Exploder, Negativist, Sherman Tank and Sniper. *Learn more about* the Universal Approaches and the Unmagnificent Seven in chapter 3, "The Arts of Aggression Management: Being Prepared."

"Us and Them" Syndrome—The innate tendency in all humans to consider their environment, nation, race, gender, geological area, etc. superior to everyone else's; a pre-judgment or prejudice.

Vasoconstriction—Narrowing or constricting of arteries and veins that supply blood to the specific areas of the aggressor's body, such as their head and hands.

Verbal Aggression Scale—In the Escalation Phase, during interpersonal communications, aggressors go through a process of questioning authority, refusing to do what they are asked to do, they verbally release or vent and finally they make intimidating or threatening remarks. *See also* Verbal Release. *Learn more about* Verbal Release and the Verbal Aggression Scale in the description of the Escalation Phase, Cognitive Aggression.

Verbal Release—At a point about midway along the Aggression Continuum when an aggressor cannot contain the pressure of mounting anxiety and needs to "vent" the pent up rage in a torrent of verbal abuse. *See also* Verbal Aggression Scale. *Learn more about* Verbal Release and the Verbal Aggression Scale in the description of the Escalation Phase, Cognitive Aggression.

Victim—An individual an aggressor senses as a threat and/or wishes to control.

Violence—Highest level of aggression expressed; the use of physical forces to injure themselves, somebody else or damage something; to violate, harm or damage something or someone.

Words with Power, Persuasive Tactic of—Use an individual's name, preferably the first name; "please" and "thank you" tend to motivate people; "might" and "maybe" help persuade others in a far more gentle and effective way; "don't" may not be heard within a statement and it might be heard in the brain as a positive, e.g., "Don't decide now, you can do it later if you're uncomfortable," may be heard as, "Decide now." *See also* Acceptance by Association, Assumption of the Obvious, Because, Being Credible, Continuity, Contrast, Creating Expectation, Expanding on Perspective, False Credibility, Fears, Framing, Friends, Infectious Emotions, Invoking Spite, Limited Offer, Peer Conformity, Perception as Truth, Persuasive Tactic, Power, Projected Thinking, Reciprocity, Reduced Concession, Reducing Isolation and Sharing Secrets. *Learn more about* Persuasive Tactics in chapter 5 "The Art of Persuasion, Pacing the Aggressor—Strategies."

Workplace Violence—A term used to characterize the various forms of verbal, emotional and physical abuse committed by one human against another in the workplace setting. "Violence" is often perceived as fatality or brutal crime therefore too many managers disregard its potential thinking "it won't happen to me." *See also* Aggression Management.

Bibliography

- Kenneth Adams, "What We Know about Police Use of Force," in *Use of Force by Police: Overview of National and Local Data*, by Kenneth Adams, et. al. (Washington, D.C.: U.S. Dept. of Justice, Office of Justice Programs, National Institute of Justice, 1999).
- Adapted from Robert M. Bramson, *Coping with Difficult People* (Garden City, N.Y.: Anchor Press/Doubleday, 1981). We have identified seven basic types of troublesome and potentially aggressive personalities. We call them "The Unmagnificent Seven." Each of us may, from time to time, exhibit one or more of these traits, but this is not what we are looking for. We want to focus on those individuals whose Unmagnificent personalities permeate their being, and who use those traits *habitually* as tools to control and manipulate others who work and live around them.
- Norman Cousins, *Head First: The Biology of Hope* (New York: Dutton, 1989).
- According to Antonio Damasio humans form "dispositional representations" (such as traits, values, opinions and schemas) over time, these representations are linked to "somatic markers" that register pain or pleasure when the representations are activated. A. R. Damasio, *Descartes' Error: Emotion, Reason and the Human Brain* (New York: Grosset & Dunlap, 1994).
- R. V. Denenberg, and Mark Braverman, *The Violence-Prone Workplace: A New Approach to Dealing with Hostile, Threatening and Uncivil Behavior* (Ithaca, N.Y.: ILR Press, 1999).
- The Cognitive Aggression Continuum is adapted originally from Friedrich Glasl, *Konfliktmanagement. Ein Handbuch für Führungskräfte, Beraterinnen und Berater*, 5., erweiterte Auflage (Bern: Verlag Paul Haupt, 1997). The likeness and meaning have changed significantly from the original as Dr. Byrnes redefined its purpose within the context of Aggression Management; F. Glasl is the originator and review by Thomas Jordan in *International Journal of Conflict Management*, vol. 8:2, 1997, pp. 170–174 within the Cognitive Aggression Continuum graphic which is referred to as the Escalation Model.
- Dave Grossman, and Gloria DeGaetano, *Stop Teaching Our Kids to Kill: A*

Call to Action against TV, Movie and Video Game Violence (New York: Crown, 1999).

- The Primal Aggression Continuum's measured relationship between the introduction of adrenaline into the aggressor's blood system and its effects on heart rate is adapted from the work of Lt. Col. Dave Grossman and Bruce Siddle ("Psychological Effects of Combat," in *Encyclopedia of Violence, Peace and Conflict*, ed. Lester Kurz [San Diego: Academic Press, 1999]). They have been conducting landmark studies in the area of adrenaline or epinephrine and violence. Dave Grossman has also written the Pulitzer Prize nominated book, *On Killing, the Psychological Cost of Learning to Kill in War and Society* (Boston: Little Brown, 1995).
- The initiation of the Primal Aggression Continuum measures the connection between stress/anxiety and adrenaline. It permits us to connect the insidious nature of stress/anxiety, the act of coping and, if unchecked, its ultimate conclusion: violence. Adapted from Dr. Archibald D. Hart, *Adrenaline and Stress, The Exciting New Breakthrough that Helps You Overcome Stress Damage* (Dallas, Tex.: Word, 1995).
- A potential aggressor channels his appraisal into some form of coping from the Middle French *couper*; to strike or cut. The strength of the reaction is a direct function of the value of the threat and the degree of certainty that the threat will thwart an objective or a goal. Adapted from Pierce J. Howard, *The Owner's Manual for the Brain: Everyday Applications from Mind-Brain Research*, 2d ed. (Austin, Tex.: Bard, 2000).
- Abraham H. Maslow, *Eupsychian Management: A Journal* (Homewood, Ill.: R. D. Irwin, 1965).
- Roland Ouellette, *Management of Aggressive Behavior: A Comprehensive Guide to Learning How to Recognize, Reduce, Manage, and Control Aggressive Behavior* (Powers Lake, Wis.: Performance Dimensions, 1993).
- Judy Suiter, and Bill J. Bonnstetter, "Individual Coping Strategies and Behavioral Style," in *Pleasure and Quality of Life*, ed. David Warburton and Neil Sherwood (New York: John Wiley, 1996).
- George J. Thompson, and Jerry B. Jenkins, *Verbal Judo: The Gentle Art of Persuasion* (New York: W. Morrow, 1993).
- Neal Trautman, *The Cutting Edge of Police Integrity* (The National Institute of Ethics).
- Focused aggression is accompanied by higher than normal levels of testosterone and is characterized by partially suppressed cortical arousal; therefore, both creativity and problem-solving ability are reduced. Adapted from Redford Williams, *The Trusting Heart: Great News about Type A Behavior* (New York: Time, 1989).
- Morris M. Womack, and Hayden H. Finely, *Communication—A Unique Significance for Law Enforcement* (Springfield, Ill.: C. C. Thomas, 1986).

About the Author

JOHN D. BYRNES, D.HUM., coined the phrase "Aggression Management" and has conducted workshops for some of the nation's largest employers (USPS, NASA, USDA, Disney Development, Safe Schools of Mississippi) with success in both diminishing aggression and increasing productivity. Organizations come to Dr. Byrnes because he is the leading authority on preventing aggression in the workplace and in schools. Dr. Byrnes has been interviewed by or published articles for the *Wall Street Journal*; *Business Insurance*; *Professional Safety* (ASSE); *Risk Management Magazine* (RIMS); *HRMagazine* (SHRM); *Controller Magazine*; *Public Risk Magazine* (PRIMA); *Occupational Health & Safety*; *News & Views* (Texas Association of School Boards Risk Management Fund); *InSights* (The Aon Risk Services Risk Management and Insurance Review); Reuters Wire Service; Knight-Ridder Newspapers; Workplace Violence Prevention Reporter (James Publishing); *Today*, Gannett Suburban Newspapers; *Yomiuri Shimbun*; *Sun-Sentinel*; the *Miami Herald*; the *Orlando Sentinel*; the *Atlanta Journal*; *St. Petersburg Times, Floridian*; and spoken before many National Associations: RIMS (Risk & Insurance Management Society), VPPPA (Voluntary Protection Programs Participants' Association), NASB (National Association of School Boards), TASB (Texas Association of School Boards), ASIS (American Society of Industrial Security), Alliance for American Insurers, ASLET (American Society of Law Enforcement Trainers), AIA (American Insurance Association), AORN (Association of Operating Room Nurses). Dr. Byrnes was selected by the U.S. Department of Labor to represent the United States at the Tri-National (Canada, Mexico and United States) Conference on Violence as a Workplace Risk Conference held in Montreal, Canada."

About the Collaborators

I wish to thank the following collaborators, whose contribution and expertise have added immeasurably to this work:

DEWEY BLACKLEDGE, ED.D. is the director of the Safe School Center since 1998. Dr. Blackledge has also served as director of the Regional Education Service Center at the University of Southern Mississippi since its inception three years ago. Both centers provide training to school personnel to enable them to raise Mississippi education standards, and to prepare teachers for the demands being made on educators for the safety and well-being of school children.

Through the Regional Education Service Center and the Mississippi Safe School Center some of the following conferences and training have been provided: the "Southeastern Regional Safe and Alternative Schools Conference," "Mississippi Safe Schools Conference," Aggression Management workshops (including Trainer-of-Trainers workshops), School Resource Officer training programs, Legal Issues Gangs and Cults, National Organization for Victims Assistance (NOVA) Crisis Response Training, as well as Orientation to National Board Certification. He is also a Certified Aggression Management instructor.

DAVID BODIE, M.A., retired from the Montgomery County, Maryland, Department of Police in 1997. During Mr. Bodie's 23 years with the Montgomery County Police he served in a variety of positions including: executive assistant to the Chief of Police, director of the Office of Staff Inspections, accreditation manager, deputy district commander, commander of the Silver Spring Community Policing Unit, shift commander, academy instructor and patrol officer. Upon his retirement,

Mr. Bodie founded Bodie Consulting Services, which provides management and training services to the public safety community.

David regularly serves as a consultant for the International Criminal Investigative Training Assistance Program (ICITAP) of the U.S. Department of Justice. As an ICITAP consultant, he has developed and delivered training programs and has provided on-site consulting services to police forces in Europe, Central Asia and South America. As an ICITAP consultant, he developed a comprehensive "Police Academy Building Program" that consisted of a two-week instructor course, a two-week curriculum design course, a one-week training evaluation course, and a two-week training manager's course. These courses, which have been translated into numerous languages, constitute the core curriculum in ICITAP'S initiative to support foreign law enforcement agencies through improving the professionalism of their police academies. Additionally, Mr. Bodie provides training services to the International Training Units of the Federal Bureau of Investigation and the U.S. Drug Enforcement Agency. He has developed and presents a course on the role of human dignity and human rights in law enforcement. Mr. Bodie has also presented training programs at the U.S. Department of Justice's International Law Enforcement Academy for Eastern Europe in Budapest, Hungary.

David also provides consulting and training assistance in the areas of supervisory leadership, executive development, change management, operational and strategic planning, team building, organizational communications and community policing. He was a featured speaker at the National Community Policing Conference in Portland, Oregon, where he did a presentation entitled "Managing the Change Process." In 1999, David was a featured speaker at the International Seminar for Law Enforcement Training in the Americas. This seminar was given in Sao Paulo, Brazil, and David's topic was "The Role of Technology in Law Enforcement Training."

In 1972, David graduated from Indiana University with a Bachelor of Arts degree in police administration. In 1982, he was awarded a Master of Arts degree in forensic science from Antioch University. Mr. Bodie is also an adjunct faculty member of Howard Community College. His teaching assignments include a variety of criminal justice courses. David is also a Certified Aggression Management instructor.

David is a member of the Fraternal Order of Police, the American Society of Law Enforcement Trainers, the American Society for Training and Development and The Institute of Management Consultants.

JIM BULLARD is a freelance writer based in Orlando whose writing style and influence can be felt throughout this book. In addition to various film and video credits, he has written extensively for the Center for Aggression Management. Jim has attended numerous Aggression Management workshops and walks the path of an Aggression Manager. In addition, he served as collaborating writer for *Building Your Own Guthrie*, an entrepreneurial success book by Daniel S. Peña; and *Setting Places, How Family Dining Can Nourish Success*, by Karen Beerbower.

DR. CHARLES W. COKER, PH.D., holds two earned and three honorary doctorates. His educational expertise ranges from psychometrics to ancient philosophies and theology. He holds professional designations as a: Certified Master Motivational Trainer, Certified Professional Behavioral Analyst, Certified Professional Values Analyst, Certified in the Myers-Briggs Type Indicator and is a Certified Aggression Management Instructor. He is also chair of the President's Council for the National Speaker's Association, president-elect of the North Florida Professional Speakers Association and was voted "Speaker of the Year" (1999–2000). Dr. Coker understands discipline and brings a unique perspective to each endeavor he undertakes. He is a Master Black Belt (5th Degree) in Tae Kwon Do and two-time U.S. Silver Medallist. He is also a Vietnam era Marine Corps officer. Dr. Chuck Coker and the staff at LifeThrive are committed to helping companies around the world become more successful by providing the people who make up those companies with tools and answers for living a more fulfilled life! Chuck's wisdom regarding the connection between aggression and productivity and his advocacy has helped immeasurably in the evolution of the Center for Aggression Management.

Dr. Coker is an expert in the analysis of how behavior, attitudes and motivations impact corporate performance issues. He has, to my knowledge, completed the greatest variety and most accurate surveys concerning this matter of any consultant in the world. He is president of LifeThrive Performance Systems, Inc. (Jacksonville, Florida) He and his staff possess a strong background in psychometrics, instrumentation and their uses in the corporate environment. Dr. Coker was part of the team conducting the landmark study on the motivations that accompany the aggressive and violent mindset (Martin, UMKC, 1998). Their expertise has been used in the development of multiple surveys that assess costs of workplace aggression, as well as other factors critical to the profitability of corporate America and the impact of the "Human Factor." The LifeThrive staff is also uniquely qualified for this purpose in that they have conducted major studies for multinational insurance organizations to isolate the causes of excessive costs due to human resource and safety issues. They have additionally reviewed the Aggression Management training and materials for behavioral applicability and accuracy. For the purpose of his chapter we use the results of their work to illustrate how several large companies identified the staggering costs associated with workplace aggression.

DENNIS JONES, R.N., M.S. has worked in health care for almost 30 years, 25 of which as a registered nurse. His primary clinical area of interest has been emergency, trauma and critical care, wherein he has worked at the Shock Trauma Center at the University of Maryland Medical Center and on the Inter-hospital Critical Care Transport team at the Johns Hopkins Hospital in Baltimore, Maryland. He received his master's degree in 1994 in trauma/critical care nursing from the University of Maryland at Baltimore School of Nursing. Additionally, he served his local community for over 21 years as a volunteer EMT-Paramedic. As a manager for a greater than 60,000 visits-per-year Emergency Department from 1994–1997, he experienced firsthand how violence was affecting his employees on a daily basis. It was during this time, due to the increased violence toward his staff, he began to develop his interest in workplace violence and Aggression Management. Dennis has attended several programs on Workplace Violence and was certified as an instructor in Aggression Management from the Center for Aggression Management in October of 2000. Lastly, Dennis has been training in martial arts for many years and holds the rank of Shodan (Black Belt) in Budoshin Jujitsu through the American Jujitsu Association.

DR. DENNIS J. KOWALSKI, ED.D., has been an educator for the past 33 years. He received his undergraduate degree in biology at Kent State University. He completed certification requirements and a master's degree in educational administration at Cleveland State University and his doctorate at the University of Akron with a cognate area of study of psychology. He was an elementary classroom teacher having experience in grades 1–6 during a five-year period at the beginning of his career. He was a building principal for 17 years serving as an elementary, middle and secondary principal. He was assistant superintendent in the Strongsville City Schools for four years, after which he was appointed superintendent where he currently serves the Strongsville School community in Strongsville, Ohio.

During his experiences, he spent time in the Cleveland City Schools and a bordering suburb, Warrensville Heights. His career spans experiences in the urban, low-income areas, as well as his current position in a middle to upper middle class suburb.

After completing his doctorate at the University of Akron, he was asked to teach part time. He has continued to teach as an adjunct professor at the University of Akron, Cleveland State University, and Ashland University since 1988. His teaching includes graduate studies in learning and leadership courses. As Dr. K puts it, "His contact with graduate students is on the cutting edge."

FRANK T. READUS has trained numerous employees during a 34-year career in the public sector. His most recent position as manager of training for the U.S. Postal Service (14,000 employees) capped a long, successful career as a trainer and instructor in the field of organization, training and development. Mr. Readus is now engaged in management consulting and teaching at the Keller Graduate School of Management. He has enhanced this experience with studies in public management, change management and organizational development at Northeastern Illinois University and Johns Hopkins University. Educational credentials consist of a M.S. in applied behavioral science, Johns Hopkins University, a B.A. in public administration, Northeastern Illinois University, coupled with a series of certifications ranging from team and group facilitation, measurement and evaluation, neurolinguistics programming to team and group facilitation.